Samuel Johnson

Political Tracts

Samuel Johnson

Political Tracts

ISBN/EAN: 9783744709460

Printed in Europe, USA, Canada, Australia, Japan

Cover: Foto ©Suzi / pixelio.de

More available books at **www.hansebooks.com**

POLITICAL

T R A C T S.

CONTAINING,

THE FALSE ALARM.
FALKLAND's ISLANDS.
THE PATRIOT; and,
TAXATION NO TYRANNY.

Fallitur, egregio quiſquis ſub principe credit
Servitium, nunquam Libertas gratior extat
Quam ſub Rege pio. CLAUDIANUS.

LONDON:
Printed for W. STRAHAN; and T. CADELL in the Strand.
MDCCLXXVI.

THE

FALSE ALARM.

[1770.]

THE

FALSE ALARM.

ONE of the chief advantages derived by the present generation from the improvement and diffusion of Philosophy, is deliverance from unnecessary terrours, and exemption from false alarms. The unusual appearances, whether regular or accidental, which once spread consternation over ages of ignorance, are now the recreations of inquisitive security. The sun is no more lamented when it is eclipsed, than when it sets; and meteors play their coruscations without prognostick or prediction.

The advancement of political knowledge may be expected to produce in time the like effects. Causeless discontent and seditious violence will grow less frequent, and less formidable, as the science of Government is better ascertained by a diligent study of the theory of Man.

It is not indeed to be expected, that physical and political truth should meet with equal acceptance, or gain ground upon the world with equal facility. The notions of the naturalist find mankind in a state of neutrality, or at worst have nothing to encounter but prejudice and vanity; prejudice without malignity, and vanity without interest. But the politician's improvements are opposed by every passion that can exclude conviction or suppress it; by ambition, by avarice, by hope, and by terrour, by public faction, and private animosity.

IT is evident, whatever be the cauſe, that this nation, with all its renown for ſpeculation and for learning, has yet made little proficiency in civil wiſdom. We are ſtill ſo much unacquainted with our own ſtate, and ſo unſkilful in the purſuit of happineſs, that we ſhudder without danger, complain without grievances, and ſuffer our quiet to be diſturbed, and our commerce to be interrupted, by an oppoſition to the government, raiſed only by intereſt, and ſupported only by clamour, which yet has ſo far prevailed upon ignorance and timidity, that many favour it as reaſonable, and many dread it as powerful.

WHAT is urged by thoſe who have been ſo induſtrious to ſpread ſuſpicion, and incite fury from one end of the kingdom to the other, may be known by peruſing the papers which have been at once preſented as petitions to the King, and exhibited in print as remonſtrances to the people. It may therefore not be improper to lay before the Public the reflections of a man who cannot favour the oppoſition, for he thinks it wicked, and cannot fear it, for he thinks it weak.

THE grievance which has produced all this tempeſt of outrage, the oppreſſion in which all other oppreſſions are included, the invaſion which has left us no property, the alarm that ſuffers no patriot to ſleep in quiet, is compriſed in a vote of the Houſe of Commons, by which the freeholders of Middleſex are deprived of a Briton's birth-right, repreſentation in parliament.

THEY have indeed received the uſual writ of election, but that writ, alas! was malicious mockery; they were inſulted with

with the form, but denied the reality, for there was one man excepted from their choice.

Non de vi, neque cæde, nec veneno,
Sed lis eſt mihi de tribus capellis.

THE character of the man thus fatally excepted, I have no purpoſe to delineate. Lampoon itſelf would diſdain to ſpeak ill of him of whom no man ſpeaks well. It is ſufficient that he is expelled the Houſe of Commons, and confined in jail as being legally convicted of ſedition and impiety.

THAT this man cannot be appointed one of the guardians and counſellors of the church and ſtate, is a grievance not to be endured. Every lover of liberty ſtands doubtful of the fate of poſterity, becauſe the chief county in England cannot take its repreſentative from a jail.

Whence Middlesex should obtain the right of being denominated the chief county, cannot easily be discovered; it is indeed the county where the chief city happens to stand, but how that city treated the favourite of Middlesex, is not yet forgotten. The county, as distinguished from the city, has no claim to particular consideration.

That a man was in jail for sedition and impiety, would, I believe, have been within memory a sufficient reason why he should not come out of jail a legislator. This reason, notwithstanding the mutability of fashion, happens still to operate on the House of Commons. Their notions, however strange, may be justified by a common observation, that few are mended by imprisonment, and that he whose crimes have made confinement necessary, seldom makes any other use of his enlarge-

ment,

ment, than to do with greater cunning what he did before with leſs.

But the people have been told with great confidence, that the Houſe cannot control the right of conſtituting repreſentatives; that he who can perſuade lawful electors to chuſe him, whatever be his character, is lawfully choſen, and has a claim to a ſeat in Parliament, from which no human authority can depoſe him.

Here, however, the patrons of oppoſition are in ſome perplexity. They are forced to confeſs, that by a train of precedents ſufficient to eſtabliſh a cuſtom of Parliament, the Houſe of Commons has juriſdiction over its own members; that the whole has power over individuals; and that this power has been exerciſed ſometimes in impriſonment, and often in expulſion.

THAT such power should reside in the House of Commons in some cases, is inevitably necessary, since it is required by every polity, that where there is a possibility of offence, there should be a possibility of punishment. A member of the House cannot be cited for his conduct in Parliament before any other court; and therefore, if the House cannot punish him, he may attack with impunity the rights of the people, and the title of the King.

THIS exemption from the authority of other courts was, I think, first established in favour of the five members in the long parliament. It is not to be considered as an usurpation, for it is implied in the principles of government. If legislative powers are not co-ordinate, they cease in part to be legislative; and if they be co-ordinate, they are unaccountable; for to whom must that power account, which has no superiour?

THE House of Commons is indeed dissoluble by the King, as the nation has of late been very clamorously told; but while it subsists it is co-ordinate with the other powers, and this co-ordination ceases only when the House by dissolution ceases to subsist.

As the particular representatives of the people are in their public character above the control of the courts of law, they must be subject to the jurisdiction of the House, and as the House, in the exercise of its authority, can be neither directed nor restrained, its own resolutions must be its laws, at least, if there is no antecedent decision of the whole legislature.

THIS privilege, not confirmed by any written law or positive compact, but by the resistless power of political necessity, they have exercised, probably from their first institution, but certainly, as their records inform us, from the 23d of Elizabeth, when they expelled a member for derogating from their privileges.

It may perhaps be doubted, whether it was originally neceſſary, that this right of control and puniſhment, ſhould extend beyond offences in the exerciſe of parliamentary duty, ſince all other crimes are cognizable by other courts. But they, who are the only judges of their own rights, have exerted the power of expulſion on other occaſions, and when wickedneſs arrived at a certain magnitude, have conſidered an offence againſt ſociety as an offence againſt the Houſe.

They have therefore diveſted notorious delinquents of their legiſlative character, and delivered them up to ſhame or puniſhment, naked and unprotected, that they might not contaminate the dignity of Parliament.

It is allowed that a man attainted of felony cannot ſit in Parliament, and the Commons probably judged, that not being bound to the forms of law, they might treat theſe as felons, whoſe crimes were in their opinion equivalent to felony; and that as a known felon could not be choſen, a man ſo like a felon, that he could not eaſily be diſtinguiſhed, ought to be expelled.

The firſt laws had no law to enforce them, the firſt authority was conſtituted by itſelf. The power exerciſed by the Houſe of Commons is of this kind, a power rooted in the principles of government, and branched out by occaſional practice; a power which neceſſity made juſt, and precedents have made legal.

It will occur that authority thus uncontrolable may, in times of heat and conteſt, be oppreſſively and injuriouſly exerted, and that he who ſuffers injuſtice, is without redreſs, however innocent, however miſerable.

THE poſition is true but the argument is uſeleſs. The Commons muſt be controlled, or be exempt from control. If they are exempt they may do injury which cannot be redreſſed, if they are controlled they are no longer legiſlative.

IF the poſſibility of abuſe be an argument againſt authority, no authority ever can be eſtabliſhed; if the actual abuſe deſtroys its legality, there is no legal government now in the world.

THIS power, which the Commons have ſo long exerciſed, they ventured to uſe once more againſt Mr. Wilkes, and on the 3d of February, 1769, expelled him the Houſe, *for having printed and publiſhed a ſeditious libel, and three obſcene and impious libels.*

If these imputations were juſt, the expulſion was ſurely ſeaſonable, and that they were juſt, the Houſe had reaſon to determine, as he had confeſſed himſelf, at the bar, the author of the libel which they term ſeditious, and was convicted in the King's Bench of both the publications.

But the Freeholders of Middleſex were of another opinion. They either thought him innocent, or were not offended by his guilt. When a writ was iſſued for the election of a knight for Middleſex, in the room of John Wilkes, Eſq; expelled the Houſe, his friends on the ſixteenth of February choſe him again.

On the 17th, it was reſolved, *that* John Wilkes, Eſq; *having been in this Seſſion of Parliament expelled the Houſe, was, and is, incapable of being elected a member to ſerve in this preſent Parliament.*

As there was no other candidate, it was resolved, at the same time, that the election of the sixteenth was a void election.

The Freeholders still continued to think that no other man was fit to represent them, and on the sixteenth of March elected him once more. Their resolution was now so well known, that no opponent ventured to appear.

The Commons began to find, that power without materials for operation can produce no effect. They might make the election void for ever, but if no other candidate could be found, their determination could only be negative. They, however, made void the last election, and ordered a new writ.

On the thirteenth of April was a new election, at which Mr. Lutterel, and others, offered themselves candidates. Every method

thod of intimidation was uſed, and ſome acts of violence were done to hinder Mr. Lutterel from appearing. He was not deterred, and the poll was taken, which exhibited for Mr. Wilkes, — — 1143

Mr. Lutterel, — — 296

The ſheriff returned Mr. Wilkes, but the Houſe, on April the fifteenth, determined that Mr. Lutterel was lawfully elected.

FROM this day begun the clamour, which has continued till now. Thoſe who had undertaken to oppoſe the miniſtry, having no grievance of greater magnitude, endeavoured to ſwell this deciſion into bulk, and diſtort it into deformity, and then held it out to terrify the nation.

EVERY artifice of ſedition has been ſince practiſed to awaken diſcontent and inflame indignation. The papers of every day have been filled with the exhortations and menaces of faction. The madneſs has ſpread

through

through all ranks and through both ſexes; women and children have clamoured for Mr. Wilkes, honeſt ſimplicity has been cheated into fury, and only the wiſe have eſcaped infection.

THE greater part may juſtly be ſuſpected of not believing their own poſition, and with them it is not neceſſary to diſpute. They cannot be convinced, who are convinced already, and it is well known that they will not be aſhamed.

THE deciſion, however, by which the ſmaller number of votes was preferred to the greater, has perplexed the minds of ſome, whoſe opinions it were indecent to deſpiſe, and who by their integrity well deſerve to have their doubts appeaſed.

EVERY diffuſe and complicated queſtion may be examined by different methods, upon different principles; and that truth,

which

which is easily found by one investigator, may be missed by another, equally honest and equally diligent.

THOSE who inquire, whether a smaller number of legal votes can elect a representative in opposition to a greater, must receive from every tongue the same answer.

THE question, therefore, must be, whether a smaller number of legal votes, shall not prevail against a greater number of votes not legal.

IT must be considered, that those votes only are legal which are legally given, and that those only are legally given, which are given for a legal candidate.

IT remains then to be discussed, whether a man expelled, can be so disqualified by a vote of the House, as that he shall be no longer eligible by lawful electors.

HERE we must again recur, not to positive institutions, but to the unwritten law of social nature, to the great and pregnant principle of political necessity. All government supposes subjects, all authority implies obedience. To suppose in one the right to command what another has the right to refuse is absurd and contradictory. A state so constituted must rest for ever in motionless equipoise, with equal attractions of contrary tendency, with equal weights of power balancing each other.

LAWS which cannot be enforced, can neither prevent nor rectify disorders. A sentence which cannot be executed can have no power to warn or to reform. If the Commons have only the power of dismissing for a few days the man whom his consti-

tuents

tuents can immediately ſend back; if they can expel but cannot exclude, they have nothing more than nominal authority, to which perhaps obedience never may be paid.

The repreſentatives of our anceſtors had an opinion very different: they fined and imprisoned their members; on great provocation they diſabled them for ever, and this power of pronouncing perpetual diſability is maintained by Selden himſelf.

These claims ſeem to have been made and allowed, when the conſtitution of our government had not yet been ſufficiently ſtudied. Such powers are not legal, becauſe they are not neceſſary; and of that power which only neceſſity juſtifies, no more is to be admitted than neceſſity obtrudes.

The Commons cannot make laws, they can only paſs reſolutions, which, like all reſolutions, are of force only to thoſe that make them, and to thoſe only while they are willing to obſerve them.

The vote of the Houſe of Commons has therefore only ſo far the force of a law, as that force is neceſſary to preſerve the vote from loſing its efficacy, it muſt begin by operating upon themſelves, and extends its influence to others, only by conſequences ariſing from the firſt intention. He that ſtarts game on his own manor, may purſue it into another.

They can properly make laws only for themſelves: a member, while he keeps his ſeat, is ſubject to theſe laws; but when he is expelled, the juriſdiction ceaſes, for he is now no longer within their dominion.

THE disability, which a vote can superinduce to expulsion, is no more than was included in expulsion itself; it is only a declaration of the Commons, that they will permit no longer him whom they thus censure to sit with them in Parliament; a declaration made by that right which they necessarily possess, of regulating their own House, and of inflicting punishment on their own delinquents.

THEY have therefore no other way to enforce the sentence of incapacity, than that of adhering to it. They cannot otherwise punish the candidate so disqualified for offering himself, nor the electors for accepting him. But if he has any competitor, that competitor must prevail, and if he has none, his election will be void; for the right of the House to reject, annihilates with regard to the man so rejected the right of electing.

IT has been urged, that the power of the House terminates with their ſeſſion; ſince a priſoner committed by the Speaker's warrant cannot be detained during the receſs. That power indeed ceaſes with the ſeſſion, which muſt operate by the agency of others, becauſe, when they do not ſit, they can employ no agent, having no longer any legal exiſtence; but that which is exerciſed on themſelves revives at their meeting, when the ſubject of that power ſtill ſubſiſts. They can in the next ſeſſion refuſe to re-admit him, whom in the former ſeſſion they expelled.

THAT expulſion inferred excluſion, in the preſent caſe, muſt be, I think, eaſily admitted. The expulſion and the writ iſſued for a new election were in the ſame ſeſſion, and ſince the Houſe is by the rule of Parliament bound for the ſeſſion by a vote once paſſed, the expelled member cannot be admitted. He that cannot be admitted, cannot be elected, and the votes given to a man ineligible being given in vain, the highest number for an eligible candidate becomes a majority.

To these conclusions, as to most moral, and to all political positions, many objections may be made. The perpetual subject of political disquisition is not absolute, but comparative good. Of two systems of government, or two laws relating to the same subject, neither will ever be such as theoretical nicety would desire, and therefore neither can easily force its way against prejudice and obstinacy; each will have its excellencies and defects, and every man, with a little help from pride, may think his own the best.

It seems to be the opinion of many, that expulsion is only a dismission of the representative to his constituents, with such a testimony against him as his sentence may comprise; and that if his constituents, notwithstanding the censure of the House, thinking his case hard, his fault trifling, or his excellencies such as overbalance it, should again chuse him as still worthy of their trust, the House cannot refuse him, for his punishment has purged his fault, and the right of electors must not be violated.

This is plausible but not cogent. It is a scheme of representation, which would make a specious appearance in a political romance, but cannot be brought into practice among us, who see every day the towering head of speculation bow down unwillingly to groveling experience.

Governments formed by chance, and gradually improved by such expedients, as the successive discovery of their defects happened to suggest, are never to be tried by a regular theory. They are fabricks of dissimilar

dissimilar materials, raised by different architects, upon different plans. We must be content with them as they are; should we attempt to mend their disproportions, we might easily demolish, and difficultly rebuild them.

Laws are now made, and customs are established; these are our rules, and by them we must be guided.

It is uncontrovertibly certain, that the Commons never intended to leave electors the liberty of returning them an expelled member, for they always require one to be chosen in the room of him that is expelled, and I see not with what propriety a man can be rechosen in his own room.

Expulsion, if this were its whole effect, might very often be desirable. Sedition, or obscenity, might be no greater crimes in the opinion of other electors, than in

that

that of the freeholders of Middlesex; and many a wretch, whom his colleagues should expel, might come back persecuted into fame, and provoke with harder front a second expulsion.

MANY of the representatives of the people can hardly be said to have been chosen at all. Some by inheriting a borough inherit a seat; and some sit by the favour of others, whom perhaps they may gratify by the act which provoked the expulsion. Some are safe by their popularity, and some by their alliances. None would dread expulsion, if this doctrine were received, but those who bought their elections, and who would be obliged to buy them again at a higher price.

BUT as uncertainties are to be determined by things certain, and customs to be explained, where it is possible, by written law, the patriots have triumphed with a quotation from an act of the *4th* and *5th* of *Anne*, which permits thoſe to be rechoſen, whoſe ſeats are vacated by the acceptance of a place of profit. This they wiſely conſider as an expulſion, and from the permiſſion, in this caſe, of a re-election, infer that every other expulſion leaves the delinquent entitled to the ſame indulgence. This is the paragraph.

" If any perſon, *being choſen a member*
" of the Houſe of Commons, ſhall accept
" of any office from the crown, *during*
" *ſuch time as he ſhall continue a member*,
" his election ſhall be, and is hereby de-
" clared to be void, and a new writ ſhall
" iſſue for a new election, as if ſuch per-
" ſon ſo accepting was naturally dead.
" *Nevertheleſs ſuch perſon ſhall be capable*
" *of being again elected*, as if his place
" had not become void as aforeſaid."

How this favours the doctrine of re-admiſſion by a ſecond choice, I am not able to diſcover. The ſtatute of 30 Ch. II. had enacted, That *he who ſhould ſit in the Houſe of Commons, without taking the oaths and ſubſcribing the teſt, ſhould be diſabled to ſit in the Houſe during that Parliament, and a writ ſhould iſſue for the election of a new member, in place of the member ſo diſabled, as if ſuch member had naturally died.*

THIS laſt clauſe is apparently copied in the act of Anne, but with the common fate of imitators. In the act of Charles, the political death continued during the Parliament, in that of Anne it was hardly worth the while to kill the man whom the next breath was to revive. It is, however, apparent, that in the opinion of the Parliament, the dead-doing lines would have kept him motionleſs, if he had not been recovered by a kind exception. A ſeat va-

cated,

cated, could not be regained without express permission of the same statute.

THE right of being chosen again to a seat thus vacated, is not enjoyed by any general right, but required a special clause, and solicitous provision.

BUT what resemblanee can imagination conceive between one man vacating his seat, by a mark of favour from the crown, and another driven from it for sedition and obscenity. The acceptance of a place contaminates no character; the crown that gives it, intends to give with it always dignity, sometimes authority. The commons, it is well known, think not worse of themselves or others for their offices of profit; yet profit implies temptation, and may expose a representative to the suspicion of his constituents; though if they still think him worthy of their confidence, they may again elect him.

SUCH

Such is the consequence. When a man is dismissed by law to his constituents, with new trust and new dignity, they may, if they think him incorruptible, restore him to his seat; what can follow, therefore, but that when the House drives out a varlet with public infamy, he goes away with the like permission to return.

If infatuation be, as the proverb tells us, the forerunner of destruction, how near must be the ruin of a nation that can be incited against it's governors, by sophistry like this. I may be excused if I catch the panick, and join my groans at this alarming crisis, with the general lamentation of weeping patriots.

Another objection is, that the Commons, by pronouncing the sentence of disqualification, make a law, and take upon themselves the power of the whole legislature. Many quotations are then pro-

duced

duced to prove that the Houſe of Commons can make no laws.

THREE acts have been cited, diſabling members for different terms on different occaſions, and it is profoundly remarked, that if the Commons could by their own privilege have made a diſqualification, their jealouſy of their privileges would never have admitted the concurrent ſanction of the other powers.

I MUST for ever remind theſe puny controvertiſts, that thoſe acts are laws of permanent obligation: that two of them are now in force, and that the other expired only when it had fulfilled its end. Such laws the Commons cannot make; they could, perhaps, have determined for themſelves, that they would expel all who ſhould not take the teſt, but they could leave no authority behind them, that ſhould oblige the next Parliament to expel them. They could refuſe the South Sea directors, but they could not entail the refuſal. They can diſqualify by vote, but not by law; they cannot know that the ſentence of diſqualification pronounced to-day may not become void to-morrow, by the diſſolution of their own Houſe. Yet while the ſame Parliament ſits, the diſqualification continues unleſs the vote be reſcinded, and while it ſo continues, makes the votes, which freeholders may give to the interdicted candidate, uſeleſs and dead, ſince there cannot exiſt, with reſpect to the ſame ſubject at the ſame time, an abſolute power to chuſe and an abſolute power to reject.

In 1614, the attorney-general was voted incapable of a ſeat in the Houſe of Commons, and the nation is triumphantly told, that though the vote never was revoked, the attorney-general is now a member. He certainly may now be a member without revocation of the vote. A law is of

perpetual

perpetual obligation, but a vote is nothing when the voters are gone. A law is a compact reciprocally made by the legiſlative powers, and therefore not to be abrogated but by all the parties. A vote is ſimply a reſolution, which binds only him that is willing to be bound.

I HAVE thus punctiliouſly and minutely, perſued this diſquiſition, becauſe I ſuſpect that theſe reaſoners, whoſe buſineſs is to deceive others, have ſometimes deceived themſelves, and I am willing to free them from their embarraſſment, though I do not expect much gratitude for my kindneſs.

OTHER objections are yet remaining, for of political objections there cannot eaſily be an end. It has been obſerved, that vice is no proper cauſe of expulſion, for if the worſt man in the Houſe were always to be expelled, in time none would be left.

But no man is expelled for being worſt, he is expelled for being enormouſly bad; his conduct is compared, not with that of others, but with the rule of action.

The puniſhment of expulſion being in its own nature uncertain, may be too great or too little for the fault.

This muſt be the caſe of many puniſhments. Forfeiture of chattels is nothing to him that has no poſſeſſions. Exile itſelf may be accidentally a good; and indeed any puniſhment leſs than death is very different to different men.

But if this precedent be admitted and eſtabliſhed, no man can hereafter be ſure that he ſhall be repreſented by him whom he would chooſe. One half of the Houſe may meet early in the morning, and ſnatch an opportunity to expel the other, and the greater part of the nation may by this

ſtratagem

ſtratagem be without its lawful repreſentatives.

He that ſees all this, ſees very far. But I can tell him of greater evils yet behind. There is one poſſibility of wickedneſs, which, at this alarming criſis, has not yet been mentioned. Every one knows the malice, the ſubtilty, the induſtry, the vigilance, and the greedineſs of the Scots. The Scotch members are about the number ſufficient to make a houſe. I propoſe it to the conſideration of the Supporters of the Bill of Rights, whether there is not reaſon to ſuſpect, that theſe hungry intruders from the North, are now contriving to expel all the Engliſh. We may then curſe the hour in which it was determined, that expulſion and excluſion are the ſame. For who can gueſs what may be done when the Scots have the whole Houſe to themſelves?

Thus agreeable to cuſtom and reaſon, notwithſtanding all objections, real or imaginary; thus conſiſtent with the practice of former times, and thus conſequential to the original principles of government, is that deciſion by which ſo much violence of diſcontent has been excited, which has been ſo dolorouſly bewailed, and ſo outrageouſly reſented.

Let us however not be ſeduced to put too much confidence in juſtice or in truth, they have often been found inactive in their own defence, and give more confidence than help to their friends and their advocates. It may perhaps be prudent to make one momentary conceſſion to falſehood, by ſuppoſing the vote in Mr. Lutterel's favour to be wrong.

All wrong ought to be rectified. If Mr. Wilkes is deprived of a lawful ſeat, both he and his electors have reaſon to complain;

complain; but it will not be eaſily found, why, among the innumerable wrongs of which a great part of mankind are hourly complaining, the whole care of the Public ſhould be transferred to Mr. Wilkes and the freeholders of Middleſex, who might all ſink into non-exiſtence, without any other effect, than that there would be room made for a new rabble, and a new retailer of ſedition and obſcenity. The cauſe of our country would ſuffer little; the rabble, whenceſoever they come, will be always patriots, and always Supporters of the Bill of Rights.

THE Houſe of Commons decides the diſputes ariſing from elections. Was it ever ſuppoſed, that in all caſes their deciſions were right? Every man whoſe lawful election is defeated, is equally wronged with Mr. Wilkes, and his conſtituents feel their diſappointment with no leſs anguiſh than the freeholders of Middleſex. Theſe decifions have often been apparently partial, and fometimes tyrannically oppreffive. A majority has been given to a favourite candidate, by expunging votes which had always been allowed, and which therefore had the authority by which all votes are given, that of cuftom uninterrupted. When the Commons determine who fhall be conftituents, they may, with fome propriety, be faid to make law, becaufe thofe determinations have hitherto, for the fake of quiet, been adopted by fucceeding Parliaments. A vote therefore of the Houfe, when it operates as a law, is to individuals a law only temporary, but to communities perpetual.

YET though all this has been done, and though at every new Parliament much of this is expected to be done again, it has never produced in any former time fuch an *alarming crifis*. We have found by experience, that though a fquire has given ale and veniſon in vain, and a borough has been compelled to ſee its deareſt intereſt in the hands of him whom it did not truſt, yet the general ſtate of the nation has continued the ſame. The ſun has riſen, and the corn has grown, and whatever talk has been of the danger of property, yet he that ploughed the field commonly reaped it, and he that built a houſe was maſter of the door: the vexation excited by injuſtice ſuffered, or ſuppoſed to be ſuffered, by any private man, or ſingle community, was local and temporary, it neither ſpread far, nor laſted long.

THE nation looked on with little care, becauſe there did not ſeem to be much danger. The conſequence of ſmall irregularities was not felt, and we had not yet learned to be terrified by very diſtant enemies.

BUT quiet and ſecurity are now at an end. Our vigilance is quickened, and our comprehenſion is enlarged. We not only ſee events in their cauſes, but before their cauſes; we hear the thunder while the ſky is clear, and ſee the mine ſprung before it is dug. Political wiſdom has, by the force of Engliſh genius, been improved at laſt not only to political intuition, but to political preſcience.

BUT it cannot, I am afraid, be ſaid, that as we are grown wiſe, we are made happy. It is ſaid of thoſe who have the wonderful power called ſecond ſight, that they ſeldom ſee any thing but evil: political ſecond ſight has the ſame effect; we hear of nothing but of an alarming criſis, of violated rights, and expiring liberties. The morning riſes upon new wrongs, and the dreamer paſſes the night in imaginary ſhackles.

THE ſphere of anxiety is now enlarged; he that hitherto cared only for himſelf, now cares for the Public; for he has learned that the happineſs of individuals is comprifed in the proſperity of the whole, and that his country never ſuffers but he ſuffers with it, however it happens that he feels no pain.

Fired with this fever of epidemic patriotiſm; the taylor ſlips his thimble, the drapier drops his yard, and the blackſmith lays down his hammer; they meet at an honeſt alehouſe, conſider the ſtate of the nation, read or hear the laſt petition, lament the miſeries of the time, are alarmed at the dreadful criſis, and ſubſcribe to the ſupport of the Bill of Rights.

It ſometimes indeed happens, that an intruder of more benevolence than prudence attempts to diſperſe their cloud of dejection, and eaſe their hearts by ſeaſonable conſolation. He tells them, that though the government cannot be too diligently watched, it may be too haſtily accuſed; and that, though private judgment is every man's right, yet we cannot judge of what we do not know; that we feel at present no evils which government can alleviate, and that the public business is committed to men who have as much right to confidence as their adversaries; that the freeholders of Middlesex, if they could not choose Mr. Wilkes, might have chosen any other man, and that *he trusts we have within the realm five hundred as good as he:* that even if this which has happened to Middlesex had happened to every other county, that one man should be made incapable of being elected, it could produce no great change in the Parliament, nor much contract the power of election; that what has been done is probably right, and that if it be wrong it is of little consequence, since a like case cannot easily occur; that expulsions are very rare, and if they should, by unbounded insolence of faction, become

more

more frequent, the electors may easily provide a second choice.

ALL this he may say, but not half of this will be heard; his opponents will stun him and themselves with a confused sound of pension and places, venality and corruption, oppression and invasion, slavery and ruin.

OUTCRIES like these, uttered by malignity, and ecchoed by folly; general accusations of indeterminate wickedness; and obscure hints of impossible designs, dispersed among those that do not know their meaning, by those that know them to be false, have disposed part of the nation, though but a small part, to pester the court with ridiculous petitions.

THE progress of a petition is well known. An ejected placeman goes down to his county or his borough, tells his friends

friends of his inability to ſerve them, and his conſtituents of the corruption of the government. His friends readily underſtand that he who can get nothing, will have nothing to give. They agree to proclaim a meeting; meat and drink are plentifully provided; a crowd is eaſily brought together, and thoſe who think that they know the reaſon of their meeting, undertake to tell thoſe who know it not. Ale and clamour unite their powers, the crowd, condenſed and heated, begins to ferment with the leven of ſedition. All ſee a thouſand evils though they cannot ſhow them, and grow impatient for a remedy, though they know not what.

A SPEECH is then made by the Cicero of the day, he ſays much, and ſuppreſſes more, and credit is equally given to what he tells, and what he conceals. The petition is read and univerſally approved. Thoſe who are ſober enough to write, add their

their names, and the reſt would ſign it if they could.

EVERY man goes home and tells his neighbour of the glories of the day; how he was conſulted and what he adviſed; how he was invited into the great room, where his lordſhip called him by his name; how he was careſſed by Sir Francis, Sir Joſeph, or Sir George; how he eat turtle and veniſon, and drank unanimity to the three brothers.

THE poor loiterer, whoſe ſhop had confined him, or whoſe wife had locked him up, hears the tale of luxury with envy, and at laſt inquires what was their petition. Of the petition nothing is remembered by the narrator, but that it ſpoke much of fears and apprehenſions, and ſomething very alarming, and that he is ſure it is againſt the government; the other is convinced that it muſt be right, and wiſhes he

had

had been there, for he loves wine and venifon, and is refolved as long as he lives to be againft the government.

The petition is then handed from town to town, and from houfe to houfe, and wherever it comes the inhabitants flock together, that they may fee that which muft be fent to the King. Names are eafily collected. One man figns becaufe he hates the papifts; another becaufe he has vowed deftruction to the turnpikes; one becaufe it will vex the parfon; another becaufe he owes his landlord nothing; one becaufe he is rich; another becaufe he is poor; one to fhew that he is not afraid, and another to fhew that he can write.

The paffage, however, is not always fmooth. Thofe who collect contributions to fedition, fometimes apply to a man of higher rank and more enlightened mind, who inftead of lending them his name, calmly

calmly reproves them for being ſeducers of the people.

You who are here, ſays he, complaining of venality, are yourſelves the agents of thoſe, who having eſtimated themſelves at too high a price, are only angry that they are not bought. You are appealing from the parliament to the rabble, and inviting thoſe, who ſcarcely, in the moſt common affairs, diſtinguiſh right from wrong, to judge of a queſtion complicated with law written and unwritten, with the general principles of government, and the particular cuſtoms of the Houſe of Commons; you are ſhewing them a grievance, ſo diſtant that they cannot ſee it, and ſo light that they cannot feel it; for how, but by unneceſſary intelligence and artificial provocation, ſhould the farmers and ſhopkeepers of Yorkſhire and Cumberland know or care how Middleſex is repreſented. Inſtead of wandering thus round the county to exaſperate the rage of party, and darken the ſuſpicions of ignorance, it is the duty of men like you, who have leiſure for inquiry, to lead back the people to their honeſt labour; to tell them, that ſubmiſſion is the duty of the ignorant, and content the virtue of the poor; that they have no ſkill in the art of government, nor any intereſt in the diſſenſions of the great; and when you meet with any, as ſome there are, whoſe underſtandings are capable of conviction, it will become you to allay this foaming ebullition, by ſhewing them that they have as much happineſs as the condition of life will eaſily receive, and that a government, of which an erroneous or unjuſt repreſentation of Middleſex is the greateſt crime that intereſt can diſcover, or malice can upbraid, is a government approaching nearer to perfection, than any that experience has known, or hiſtory related.

THE drudges of ſedition wiſh to change their ground, they hear him with ſullen ſilence, feel conviction without repentance, and are confounded but not abaſhed; they go forward to another door, and find a kinder reception from a man enraged againſt the government, becauſe he has juſt been paying the tax upon his windows.

THAT a petition for a diſſolution of the Parliament will at all times have its favourers, may be eaſily imagined. The people indeed do not expect that one Houſe of Commons will be much honeſter or much wiſer than another; they do not ſuppoſe that the taxes will be lightened; or though they have been ſo often taught to hope it, that ſoap and candles will be cheaper; they expect no redreſs of grievances, for of no grievances but taxes do they complain; they wiſh not the extenſion of liberty, for they do not feel any restraint; about the security of privilege or property they are totally careless, for they see no property invaded, nor know, till they are told, that any privilege has suffered violation.

Least of all do they expect, that any future Parliament will lessen its own powers, or communicate to the people that authority which it has once obtained.

Yet a new Parliament is sufficiently desirable. The year of election is a year of jollity; and what is still more delightful, a year of equality. The glutton now eats the delicacies for which he longed when he could not purchase them, and the drunkard has the pleasure of wine without the cost. The drone lives a-while without work, and the shopkeeper, in the flow of money, raises his price. The mechanic that trembled at the presence of Sir Joseph, now bids him come again for an anſwer; and the poacher whoſe gun has been ſeized, now finds an opportunity to reclaim it. Even the honeſt man is not diſpleaſed to ſee himſelf important, and willingly reſumes in two years that power which he had reſigned for ſeven. Few love their friends ſo well as not to deſire ſuperiority by unexpenſive benefaction.

Yet, notwithſtanding all theſe motives to compliance, the promoters of petitions have not been ſucceſsful. Few could be perſuaded to lament evils which they did not ſuffer, or to ſolicit for redreſs which they do not want. The petition has been, in ſome places, rejected; and perhaps in all but one, ſigned only by the meaneſt and groſſeſt of the people.

Since this expedient now invented or revived to diſtreſs the government, and equally practicable at all times by all who ſhall be excluded from power and from profit, has produced ſo little effect, let us conſider the oppoſition as no longer formidable. The great engine has recoiled upon them. They thought that *the terms they ſent were terms of weight*, which would have *amazed all and ſtumbled many*; but the conſternation is now over, and their foes *ſtand upright*, as before.

WITH great propriety and dignity the king has, in his ſpeech, neglected or forgotten them. He might eaſily know, that what was preſented as the ſenſe of the people, is the ſenſe only of the profligate and diſſolute; and that whatever Parliament ſhould be convened, the ſame petitioners would be ready, for the ſame reaſon, to requeſt its diſſolution.

As we once had a rebellion of the clowns, we have now an oppoſition of the pedlars. The quiet of the nation has been for

for years diſturbed by a faction, againſt which all factions ought to conſpire; for its original principle is the deſire of levelling; it is only animated under the name of zeal, by the natural malignity of the mean againſt the great.

When in the confuſion which the Engliſh invaſions produced in France, the villains, imagining that they had found the golden hour of emancipation, took arms in their hands, the knights of both nations conſidered the cauſe as common, and, ſuſpending the general hoſtility, united to chaſtiſe them.

The whole conduct of this deſpicable faction is diſtinguiſhed by plebeian groſsneſs, and ſavage indecency. To miſrepreſent the actions and the principles of their enemies is common to all parties; but the inſolence of invective, and brutality of reproach, which have lately prevailed, are peculiar to this.

An infallible characteristic of meanness is cruelty. This is the only faction that has shouted at the condemnation of a criminal, and that, when his innocence procured his pardon, has clamoured for his blood.

All other parties, however enraged at each other, have agreed to treat the throne with decency; but these low-born railers have attacked not only the authority, but the character of their Sovereign, and have endeavoured, surely without effect, to alienate the affections of the people from the only king, who, for almost a century, has much appeared to desire, or much endeavoured to deserve them. They have insulted him with rudeness and with menaces, which were never excited by the gloomy sullenness of William, even when half the nation denied him their allegiance; nor by the dangerous bigotry of James, unleſs when he was finally driven from his palace; and with which ſcarcely the open hoſtilities of rebellion ventured to vilify the unhappy Charles, even in the remarks on the cabinet of Naſeby.

It is ſurely not unreaſonable to hope, that the nation will conſult its dignity, if not its ſafety, and diſdain to be protected or enſlaved by the declaimers or the plotters of a city-tavern. Had Rome fallen by the Catilinarian conſpiracy, ſhe might have conſoled her fate by the greatneſs of her deſtroyers; but what would have alleviated the diſgrace of England, had her government been changed by Tiler or by Ket?

One part of the nation has never before contended with the other, but for ſome weighty and apparent intereſt. If the means were violent, the end was great.

The civil war was fought for what each army called and believed the beſt religion, and the beſt government. The ſtruggle in the reign of Anne, was to exclude or reſtore an exiled king. We are now diſputing, with almoſt equal animoſity, whether Middleſex ſhall be repreſented or not by a criminal from a jail.

The only comfort left in ſuch degeneracy is, that a lower ſtate can be no longer poſſible.

In this contemptuous cenſure, I mean not to include every ſingle man. In all lead, ſays the chemiſt, there is ſilver; and in all copper there is gold. But mingled maſſes are juſtly denominated by the greater quantity, and when the precious particles are not worth extraction, a faction and a pig muſt be melted down together to the forms and offices that chance allots them.

Fiunt urceoli, pelves, ſartago, patellæ.

A FEW weeks will now ſhew whether the Government can be ſhaken by empty noiſe, and whether the faction which depends upon its influence, has not deceived alike the Public and itſelf. That it ſhould have continued till now, is ſufficiently ſhameful. None can indeed wonder that it has been ſupported by the ſectaries, the natural fomenters of ſedition, and confederates of the rabble, of whoſe religion little now remains but hatred of eſtabliſhments, and who are angry to find ſeparation now only tolerated, which was once rewarded; but every honeſt man muſt lament, that it has been regarded with frigid neutrality by the Tories, who, being long accuſtomed to ſignalize their principles by oppoſition to the court, do not yet conſider that they have at laſt a king who knows not the name of party, and who wiſhes to be the common father of all his people.

As a man inebriated only by vapours, ſoon recovers in the open air; a nation diſcontented to madneſs, without any adequate cauſe, will return to its wits and its allegiance when a little pauſe has cooled it to reflection. Nothing, therefore, is neceſſary, at this *alarming criſis*, but to conſider the alarm as falſe. To make conceſſions is to encourage encroachment. Let the court deſpiſe the faction, and the diſappointed people will ſoon deride it.

THOUGHTS

ON THE

LATE TRANSACTIONS

RESPECTING

Falkland's Iflands.

FALKLAND's ISLANDS.

TO proportion the eagerness of contest to its importance seems too hard a task for human wisdom. The pride of wit has kept ages busy in the discussion of useless questions, and the pride of power has destroyed armies to gain or to keep unprofitable possessions.

Not many years have passed since the cruelties of war were filling the world with terror and with sorrow; [illegible] appeased, [illegible] and to the harassed nations [illegible] pleasures and its benefits. [illegible] all felt the happiness, and all enjoyed the ease.

FALKLAND's ISLANDS.

TO proportion the eagerneſs of conteſt to its importance ſeems too hard a taſk for human wiſdom. The pride of wit has kept ages buſy in the diſcuſſion of uſeleſs queſtions, and the pride of power has deſtroyed armies to gain or to keep unprofitable poſſeſſions.

NOT many years have paſſed ſince the cruelties of war were filling the world with terror and with ſorrow; rage was at laſt appeaſed, or ſtrength exhauſted, and to the haraſſed nations peace was reſtored, with its pleaſures and its benefits. Of this ſtate all felt the happineſs, and all implored the

con-

continuance; but what continuance of happiness can be expected, when the whole system of European empire can be in danger of a new concussion, by a contention for a few spots of earth, which, in the deserts of the ocean, had almost escaped human notice, and which, if they had not happened to make a sea-mark, had perhaps never had a name.

FORTUNE often delights to dignify what nature has neglected, and that renown which cannot be claimed by intrinsick excellence or greatness, is sometimes derived from unexpected accidents. The Rubicon was ennobled by the passage of Cæsar, and the time is now come when Falkland's Islands demand their historian.

BUT the writer to whom this employment shall be assigned, will have few opportunities of descriptive splendor, or narrative elegance. Of other countries it is told

told how often they have changed their government; these islands have hitherto changed only their name. Of heroes to conquer, or legislators to civilize, here has been no appearance; nothing has happened to them but that they have been sometimes seen by wandering navigators, who passed by them in search of better habitations.

WHEN the Spaniards, who, under the conduct of Columbus, discovered America, had taken possession of its most wealthy regions; they surprised and terrified Europe by a sudden and unexampled influx of riches. They were made at once insupportably insolent, and might perhaps have become irresistibly powerful, had not their mountainous treasures been scattered in the air with the ignorant profusion of unaccustomed opulence.

THE greater part of the European potentates saw this stream of riches flowing into Spain

Spain without attempting to dip their own hands in the golden fountain. France had no naval ſkill or power; Portugal was extending her dominions in the Eaſt over regions formed in the gaiety of Nature; the Hanſeatic league, being planned only for the ſecurity of traffick, had no tendency to diſcovery or invaſion; and the commercial ſtates of Italy growing rich by trading between Aſia and Europe, and not lying upon the ocean, did not deſire to ſeek by great hazards, at a diſtance, what was almoſt at home to be found with ſafety.

The Engliſh alone were animated by the ſucceſs of the Spaniſh navigators, to try if any thing was left that might reward adventure, or incite appropriation. They ſent Cabot into the North, but in the North there was no gold or ſilver to be found. The beſt regions were pre-occupied, yet they ſtill continued their hopes and their labours. They were the ſecond nation that dared the extent of the Pacifick Ocean, and the ſecond circumnavigators of the globe.

By the war between Elizabeth and Philip, the wealth of America became lawful prize, and thoſe who were leſs afraid of danger than of poverty, ſuppoſed that riches might eaſily be obtained by plundering the Spaniards. Nothing is difficult when gain and honour unite their influence; the ſpirit and vigour of theſe expeditions enlarged our views of the new world, and made us firſt acquainted with its remoter coaſts.

In the fatal voyage of Cavendiſh (1592) Captain Davis, who, being ſent out as his aſſociate, was afterwards parted from him or deſerted him, as he was driven by violence of weather about the Straits of Magellan, is ſuppoſed to have been the firſt who ſaw the lands now called Falkland's Iſlands, but his diſtreſs permitted him not to make any obſervation, and he left them, as he found them, without a name.

Not long afterwards (1594) Sir Richard Hawkins, being in the ſame ſeas with the ſame deſigns, ſaw theſe iſlands again, if they are indeed the ſame iſlands, and in honour of his miſtreſs, called them Hawkins's Maiden Land.

This voyage was not of renown ſufficient to procure a general reception to the new name, for when the Dutch, who had now become ſtrong enough not only to defend themſelves, but to attack their maſters, ſent (1598) Verhagen and Sebald de Wert, into the South Sea, theſe Iſlands, which were not ſuppoſed to have been known before, obtained the denomination of Sebald's Iſlands, and were from that time placed in the charts; though Frezier tells us, that they were yet conſidered as of doubtful exiſtence.

Their present English name was probably given them (1689) by Strong, whose journal, yet unprinted, may be found in the Museum. This name was adopted by Halley, and has from that time, I believe, been received into our maps.

The privateers which were put into motion by the wars of William and Anne, saw those islands and mention them; but they were yet not considered as territories worth a contest. Strong affirmed that there was no wood, and Dampier suspected that they had no water.

Frezier describes their appearance with more distinctness, and mentions some ships of St. Maloes, by which they had been visited, and to which he seems willing enough to ascribe the honour of discovering islands which yet he admits to have been seen by Hawkins, and named by Sebald de Wert. He, I suppose, in honour of his countrymen, called them the Malouines, the denomination now uſed by the Spaniards, who ſeem not, till very lately, to have thought them important enough to deſerve a name.

SINCE the publication of Anſon's voyage, they have very much changed their opinion, finding a ſettlement in Pepys's or Falkland's Iſland recommended by the author as neceſſary to the ſucceſs of our future expeditions againſt the coaſt of Chili, and as of ſuch uſe and importance, that it would produce many advantages in peace, and in war would make us maſters of the South Sea.

SCARCELY any degree of judgment is ſufficient to reſtrain the imagination from magnifying that on which it is long detained. The relator of Anſon's voyage had heated his mind with its various events, had partaken the hope with which it was begun, and the vexation ſuffered by its various miſcarriages, and then thought nothing could be of greater benefit to the nation than that which might promote the ſucceſs of ſuch another enterpriſe.

HAD the heroes of that hiſtory even performed and attained all that when they firſt ſpread their ſails they ventured to hope, the conſequence would yet have produced very little hurt to the Spaniards, and very little benefit to the Engliſh. They would have taken a few towns; Anſon and his companions would have ſhared the plunder or the ranſom; and the Spaniards, finding their ſouthern territories acce ble, would for the future have guarded them better.

THAT ſuch a ſettlement may be of uſe in war, no man that conſiders its ſituation will deny. But war is not the whole buſineſs of life; it happens but ſeldom, and every man, either good or wiſe, wiſhes that its frequency were ſtill leſs. That conduct which betrays deſigns of future hoſtility, if it does not excite violence, will always generate malignity; it muſt for ever exclude confidence and friendſhip, and continue a cold and ſluggiſh rivalry, by a ſly reciprocation of indirect injuries, without the bravery of war, or the ſecurity of peace.

THE advantage of ſuch a ſettlement in time of peace is, I think, not eaſily to be proved. For what uſe can it have but of a ſtation for contraband traders, a nurſery of fraud, and a receptacle of theft? Narborough, about a century ago, was of opinion, that no advantage could be obtained in voyages to the South Sea, except by ſuch an armament as, with a ſailor's morality, *might trade by force.* It is well known that the prohibitions of foreign commerce are, in theſe countries, to the laſt degree rigorous, and that no man not autho-

authorized by the King of Spain can trade there but by force or ſtealth. Whatever profit is obtained muſt be gained by the violence of rapine, or dexterity of fraud.

GOVERNMENT will not perhaps ſoon arrive at ſuch purity and excellence, but that ſome connivance at leaſt will be indulged to the triumphant robber and ſucceſsful cheat. He that brings wealth home is ſeldom interrogated by what means it was obtained. This, however, is one of thoſe modes of corruption with which mankind ought always to ſtruggle, and which they may in time hope to overcome. There is reaſon to expect, that as the world is more enlightened, policy and morality will at laſt be reconciled, and that nations will learn not to do what they would not ſuffer.

BUT the ſilent toleration of ſuſpected guilt is a degree of depravity far below that which openly incites and manifeſtly protects it. To pardon a pirate may be injurious to mankind; but how much greater is the crime of opening a port in which all pirates shall be safe? The contraband trader is not more worthy of protection: if with Narborough he trades by force, he is a pirate; if he trades secretly, he is only a thief. Those who honestly refuse his traffick he hates as obstructors of his profit; and those with whom he deals he cheats, because he knows that they dare not complain. He lives with a heart full of that malignity which fear of detection always generates in those who are to defend unjust acquisitions against lawful authority; and when he comes home with riches thus acquired, he brings a mind hardened in evil, too proud for reproof, and too stupid for reflection; he offends the high by his insolence, and corrupts the low by his example.

WHETHER these truths were forgotten or despised, or whether some better purpose

was

was then in agitation, the repreſentation made in Anſon's voyage had ſuch effect upon the ſtateſmen of that time, that (in 1748) ſome ſloops were fitted out for the fuller knowledge of Pepys and Falkland's Iſlands, and for further diſcoveries in the South Sea. This expedition, though perhaps deſigned to be ſecret, was not long concealed from *Wall*, the Spaniſh ambaſſador, who ſo vehemently oppoſed it, and ſo ſtrongly maintained the right of the Spaniards to the excluſive dominion of the South Sea, that the Engliſh miniſtry relinquiſhed part of their original deſign, and declared that the examination of thoſe two Iſlands was the utmoſt that their orders ſhould compriſe.

THIS conceſſion was ſufficiently liberal or ſufficiently ſubmiſſive; yet the Spaniſh court was neither gratified by our kindneſs, nor ſoftened by our humility. Sir Benjamin Keene, who then reſided at Madrid, was interrogated by Carvajal concerning the visit intended to Pepys' and Falkland's Islands in terms of great jealousy and discontent; and the intended expedition was represented, if not as a direct violation of the late peace, yet as an act inconsistent with amicable intentions, and contrary to the professions of mutual kindness which then passed between Spain and England. Keene was directed to protest that nothing more than mere discovery was intended, and that no settlement was to be established. The Spaniard readily replied, that if this was a voyage of wanton curiosity, it might be gratified with less trouble, for he was willing to communicate whatever was known: That to go so far only to come back, was no reasonable act; and it would be a slender sacrifice to peace and friendship to omit a voyage in which nothing was to be gained: That if we left the places as we found them, the voyage was useless; and if we took possession, it was a hostile armament, nor

 could

could we expect that the Spaniards would suppose us to visit the southern parts of America only from curiosity, after the scheme proposed by the author of Anson's Voyage.

WHEN once we had disowned all purpose of settling, it is apparent that we could not defend the propriety of our expedition by arguments equivalent to Carvajal's objections. The ministry therefore dismissed the whole design, but no declaration was required by which our right to persue it hereafter might be annulled.

FROM this time Falkland's Island was forgotten or neglected, till the conduct of naval affairs was intrusted to the Earl of Egmont, a man whose mind was vigorous and ardent, whose knowledge was extensive, and whose designs were magnificent; but who had somewhat vitiated his judgement by too much indulgence of romantick projects and airy speculations.

Lord Egmont's eagerneſs after ſomething new determined him to make inquiry after Falkland's Iſland, and he ſent out Captain Byron, who, in the beginning of the year 1765, took, he ſays, a formal poſſeſſion in the name of his Britannick Majeſty.

The poſſeſſion of this place is, according to Mr. Byron's repreſentation, no deſpicable acquiſition. He conceived the iſland to be ſix or ſeven hundred miles round, and repreſented it as a region naked indeed of wood, but which, if that defect were ſupplied, would have all that nature, almoſt all that luxury could want. The harbour he found capacious and ſecure, and therefore thought it worthy of the name of Egmont. Of water there was no want, and the ground, he deſcribed as having all the excellencies of ſoil, and as covered with antiſcorbutick herbs, the reſtoratives of the ſailor. Proviſion was eaſily to be had, for they kill-

ed

ed almost every day an hundred geese to each ship, by pelting them with stones. Not content with physick and with food, he searched yet deeper for the value of the new dominion. He dug in quest of ore, found iron in abundance, and did not despair of nobler metals.

A COUNTRY thus fertile and delightful, fortunately found where none would have expected it, about the fiftieth degree of southern latitude, could not without great supineness be neglected. Early in the next year (January 8, 1766) Captain Macbride arrived at Port Egmont, where he erected a small blockhouse, and stationed a garrison. His description was less flattering. He found, what he calls, a mass of islands and broken lands, of which the soil was nothing but a bog, with no better prospect than that of barren mountains, beaten by storms almost perpetual. Yet this, says he, is summer, and if the winds of winter hold their natural proportion, those who lie but two cables length from the ſhore, muſt paſs weeks without any communication with it. The plenty which regaled Mr. Byron, and which might have ſupported not only armies, but armies of Patagons, was no longer to be found. The geeſe were too wiſe to ſtay when men violated their haunts, and Mr. Macbride's crew could only now and then kill a gooſe when the weather would permit. All the quadrupeds which he met there were foxes, ſuppoſed by him to have been brought upon the ice; but of uſeleſs animals, ſuch as ſea lions and penguins, which he calls vermin, the number was incredible. He allows, however, that thoſe who touch at theſe iſlands may find geeſe and ſnipes, and in the ſummer months, wild cellery and ſorrel.

No token was ſeen by either, of any ſettlement ever made upon this iſland, and Mr. Macbride thought himſelf ſo ſecure from hoſtile diſturbance, that when he

erected

erected his wooden blockhouſe he omitted to open the ports and loopholes.

WHEN a garriſon was ſtationed at Port Egmont, it was neceſſary to try what ſuſtenance the ground could be by culture excited to produce. A garden was prepared, but the plants that ſprung up, withered away in immaturity. Some fir-ſeeds were ſown; but though this be the native tree of rugged climates, the young firs that roſe above the ground died like weaker herbage. The cold continued long, and the ocean ſeldom was at reſt.

CATTLE ſucceeded better than vegetables. Goats, ſheep, and hogs, that were carried thither, were found to thrive and increaſe as in other places.

Nil mortalibus arduum eſt. There is nothing which human courage will not undertake, and little that human patience will not endure. The garriſon lived upon Falkland's land's Island, shrinking from the blast, and shuddering at the billows.

THIS was a colony which could never become independent, for it never could be able to maintain itself. The necessary supplies were annually sent from England, at an expence which the Admiralty began to think would not quickly be repaid. But shame of deserting a project, and unwillingness to contend with a projector that meant well, continued the garrison, and supplied it with regular remittances of stores and provision.

THAT of which we were almost weary ourselves, we did not expect any one to envy; and therefore supposed that we should be permitted to reside in Falkland's Island, the undisputed lords of tempest-beaten barrenness.

BUT, on the 28th of November 1769, Captain Hunt, observing a Spanish schooner hovering

hovering about the iſland and ſurveying it, ſent the commander a meſſage, by which he required him to depart. The Spaniard made an appearance of obeying, but in two days came back with letters written by the governor of Port Solidad, and brought by the chief officer of a ſettlement on the eaſt part of Falkland's Iſland.

In this letter, dated *Malouina*, November 30, the governor complains, that Captain Hunt, when he ordered the ſchooner to depart, aſſumed a power to which he could have no pretenſions, by ſending an imperious meſſage to the Spaniards in the King of Spain's own dominions.

In another letter ſent at the ſame time, he ſuppoſes the Engliſh to be in that part only by accident, and to be ready to depart at the firſt warning. This letter was accompanied by a preſent, of which, ſays he, *if it be neither equal to my deſire nor to your merit, you must impute the deficiency to the situation of us both.*

In return to this hostile civility, Captain Hunt warned them from the island, which he claimed in the name of the King, as belonging to the English by right of the first discovery and the first settlement.

This was an assertion of more confidence than certainty. The right of discovery indeed has already appeared to be probable; but the right which priority of settlement confers I know not whether we yet can establish.

On December 10, the officer sent by the governor of Port Solidad made three protests against Captain Hunt; for threatening to fire upon him; for opposing his entrance into Port Egmont; and for entering himself into Port Solidad. On the 12th the governor of Port Solidad formally warned

Captain

Captain Hunt to leave Port Egmont; and to forbear the navigation of these seas, without permission from the King of Spain.

To this Captain Hunt replied by repeating his former claim; by declaring that his orders were to keep possession; and by once more warning the Spaniards to depart.

The next month produced more protests and more replies, of which the tenour was nearly the same. The operations of such harmless enmity having produced no effect, were then reciprocally discontinued, and the English were left for a time to enjoy the pleasures of Falkland's Island without molestation.

This tranquillity, however, did not last long. A few months afterwards (June 4, 1770) the Industry, a Spanish frigate, commanded by an officer whose name was Madariaga, anchored in Port Egmont, bound, as was said, for Port Solidad, and reduced, by a passage from Buenos Ayres of fifty-three days, to want of water.

THREE days afterwards four other frigates entered the port, and a broad pendant, such as is born by the commander of a naval armament, was displayed from the Industry. Captain Farmer of the Swift frigate, who commanded the garrison, ordered the crew of the Swift to come on shore, and assist in its defence; and directed Captain Maltby to bring the Favourite frigate, which he commanded, nearer to the land. The Spaniards easily discovering the purpose of his motion, let him know, that if he weighed his anchor, they would fire upon his ship; but paying no regard to these menaces, he advanced towards the shore. The Spanish fleet followed, and two shots were fired, which fell at a distance from him. He then sent to inquire the reason of such hostility, and was told

told that the shots were intended only as signals.

BOTH the English captains wrote the next day to Madariaga the Spanish commodore, warning him from the island, as from a place which the English held by right of discovery.

MADARIAGA, who seems to have had no desire of unnecessary mischief, invited them (June 9.) to send an officer who should take a view of his forces, that they might be convinced of the vanity of resistance, and do that without compulsion which he was upon refusal prepared to enforce.

AN officer was sent, who found sixteen hundred men, with a train of twenty-seven cannon, four mortars, and two hundred bombs. The fleet consisted of five frigates from twenty to thirty guns, which were now stationed opposite to the Block-house.

He then ſent them a formal memorial, in which he maintained his maſter's right to the whole Magellanick region, and exhorted the Engliſh to retire quietly from the ſettlement, which they could neither juſtify by right, nor maintain by power.

He offered them the liberty of carrying away whatever they were deſirous to remove, and promiſed his receipt for what ſhould be left, that no loſs might be ſuffered by them.

His propoſitions were expreſſed in terms of great civility; but he concludes with demanding an anſwer in fifteen minutes.

Having while he was writing received the letters of warning written the day before by the Engliſh captains, he told them, that he thought himſelf able to prove the King of Spain's title to all thoſe countries, but that this was no time for verbal altercations. He persisted in his determination, and allowed only fifteen minutes for an answer.

To this it was replied by Captain Farmer, that though there had been prescribed yet a shorter time, he should still resolutely defend his charge; that this, whether menace or force, would be considered as an insult on the British flag, and that satisfaction would certainly be required.

On the next day (June 10.) Madariaga landed his forces, and it may be easily imagined that he had no bloody conquest. The English had only a wooden blockhouse built at Woolwich, and carried in pieces to the island, with a small battery of cannon. To contend with obstinacy had been only to lavish life without use or hope. After the exchange of a very few shots, a capitulation was proposed.

The Spanish commander acted with moderation; he exerted little of the conqueror; what he had offered before the attack, he granted after the victory; the Engliſh were allowed to leave the place with every honour, only their departure was delayed by the terms of the capitulation twenty days; and to ſecure their ſtay, the rudder of the Favourite was taken off. What they deſired to carry away they removed without moleſtation; and of what they left an inventory was drawn, for which the Spaniſh officer by his receipt promiſed to be accountable.

Of this petty revolution, ſo ſudden and ſo diſtant, the Engliſh miniſtry could not poſſibly have ſuch notice as might enable them to prevent it. The conqueſt, if ſuch it may be called, coſt but three days; for the Spaniards, either ſuppoſing the garriſon ſtronger than it was, or reſolving to truſt nothing to chance, or conſidering that as their force was greater, there was leſs danger of bloodſhed, came with a power that made resistance ridiculous, and at once demanded and obtained possession.

THE first account of any discontent expressed by the Spaniards was brought by Captain Hunt, who arriving at Plymouth June 3, 1770, informed the Admiralty that the island had been claimed in December by the governor of Port Solidad.

THIS claim, made by an officer of so little dignity, without any known direction from his superiors, could be considered only as the zeal or officiousness of an individual, unworthy of public notice or the formality of remonstrance.

IN August Mr. Harris, the resident at Madrid, gave notice to Lord Weymouth of an account newly brought to Cadiz, that the English were in possession of Port Cuizada, the same which we call Port Egmont, in the Magellanick sea; that in

January they had warned away two Spanish ships; and that an armament was sent out in May from Buenos Ayres to dislodge them.

It was perhaps not yet certain that this account was true; but the information, however faithful, was too late for prevention. It was easily known, that a fleet dispatched in May had before August succeeded or miscarried.

In October, Captain Maltby came to England, and gave the account which I have now epitomised, of his expulsion from Falkland's Islands.

From this moment the whole nation can witness that no time was lost. The navy was surveyed, the ships refitted, and commanders appointed; and a powerful fleet was assembled, well manned and well stored, with expedition after so long a peace per-

hasp

haps never known before, and with vigour which after the waſte of ſo long a war ſcarcely any other nation had been capable of exerting.

This preparation, ſo illuſtrious in the eyes of Europe, and ſo efficacious in its event, was obſtructed by the utmoſt power of that noiſy faction which has too long filled the kingdom, ſometimes with the roar of empty menace, and ſometimes with the yell of hypocritical lamentation. Every man ſaw, and every honeſt man ſaw with deteſtation, that they who deſired to force their ſovereign into war, endeavoured at the ſame time to diſable him from action.

The vigour and ſpirit of the miniſtry eaſily broke through all the machinations of theſe pygmy rebels, and our armament was quickly ſuch as was likely to make our negociations effectual.

The Prince of Maſſeran, in his firſt conference with the Engliſh miniſters on this occaſion, owned that he had from Madrid received intelligence that the Engliſh had been forcibly expelled from Falkland's Iſland by Buccarelli, the governor of Buenos Ayres, without any particular orders from the King of Spain. But being aſked, whether in his maſter's name he diſavowed Buccarelli's violence, he refuſed to anſwer without direction.

The ſcene of negociation was now removed to Madrid, and in September Mr. Harris was directed to demand from Grimaldi the Spaniſh miniſter the reſtitution of Falkland's Iſland, and a diſavowal of Buccarelli's hoſtilities.

It was to be expected that Grimaldi would object to us our own behaviour, who had ordered the Spaniards to depart from the ſame iſland. To this it was replied, That the Engliſh forces were indeed directed to warn other nations away; but if

com-

compliance were refused, to proceed quietly in making their settlement, and suffer the subjects of whatever power to remain there without molestation. By possession thus taken, there was only a disputable claim advanced, which might be peaceably and regularly decided, without insult and without force; and if the Spaniards had complained at the British court, their reasons would have been heard, and all injuries redressed; but that, by presupposing the justice of their own title, and having recourse to arms, without any previous notice or remonstrance, they had violated the peace, and insulted the British government; and therefore it was expected that satisfaction should be made by publick disavowal and immediate restitution.

THE answer of Grimaldi was ambiguous and cold. He did not allow that any particular orders had been given for driving the English from their settlement; but made no

scruple

ſcruple of declaring, that ſuch an ejection was nothing more than the ſettlers might have expected; and that Buccarelli had not, in his opinion, incurred any blame, as the general injunctions to the American governors were, to ſuffer no incroachments on the Spaniſh dominions.

In October the Prince of Maſſeran propoſed a convention for the accommodation of differences by mutual conceſſions, in which the warning given to the Spaniards by Hunt ſhould be diſavowed on one ſide, and the violence uſed by Buccarelli on the other. This offer was conſidered as little leſs than a new inſult, and Grimaldi was told, that injury required reparation; that when either party had ſuffered evident wrong, there was not the parity ſubſiſting which is implied in conventions and contracts; that we conſidered ourſelves as openly inſulted, and demanded ſatisfaction plenary and unconditional.

GRIMALDI

GRIMALDI affected to wonder that we were not yet appeaſed by their conceſſions. They had, he ſaid, granted all that was required; they had offered to reſtore the iſland in the ſtate in which they found it; but he thought that they likewiſe might hope for ſome regard, and that the warning ſent by Hunt would be diſavowed.

MR. HARRIS, our miniſter at Madrid, inſiſted that the injured party had a right to unconditional reparation, and Grimaldi delayed his anſwer that a council might be called. In a few days orders were diſpatched to Prince Maſſeran, by which he was commiſſioned to declare the King of Spain's readineſs to ſatisfy the demands of the King of England, in expectation of receiving from him reciprocal ſatisfaction, by the diſavowal, ſo often required, of Hunt's warning.

FINDING the Spaniards diſpoſed to make no other acknowledgments, the Engliſh

miniſtry

ministry considered a war as not likely to be long avoided. In the latter end of November private notice was given of their danger to the merchants at Cadiz, and the officers absent from Gibraltar were remanded to their posts. Our naval force was every day increased, and we made no abatement of our original demand.

THE obstinacy of the Spanish court still continued, and about the end of the year all hope of reconciliation was so nearly extinguished, that Mr. Harris was directed to withdraw, with the usual forms, from his residence at Madrid.

MODERATION is commonly firm, and firmness is commonly successful; having not swelled our first requisition with any superfluous appendages, we had nothing to yield, we therefore only repeated our first proposition, prepared for war, though desirous of peace.

About this time, as is well known, the king of France dismissed Choiseul from his employments. What effect this revolution of the French court had upon the Spanish counsels, I pretend not to be informed. Choiseul had always professed pacific dispositions, nor is it certain, however it may be suspected, that he talked in different strains to different parties.

It seems to be almost the universal error of historians to suppose it politically, as it is physically true, that every effect has a proportionate cause. In the inanimate action of matter upon matter, the motion produced can be but equal to the force of the moving power; but the operations of life, whether private or publick, admit no such laws. The caprices of voluntary agents laugh at calculation. It is not always that there is a strong reason for a great event. Obstinacy and flexibility, malignity and kindness, give place alternately to each other, and the reason of these vicissitudes, however important may be the consequences, often escapes the mind in which the change is made.

WHETHER the alteration which began in January to appear in the Spanish counsels had any other cause than conviction of the impropriety of their past conduct, and of the danger of a new war, it is not easy to decide; but they began, whatever was the reason, to relax their haughtiness, and Mr. Harris's departure was countermanded.

THE demands first made by England were still continued, and on January 22d, the prince of Masseran delivered a declaration, in which the king of Spain *disavows the violent enterprise* of Buccarelli, and promises *to restore the port and fort called Egmont, with all the artillery and stores, according to the inventory.*

To this promise of restitution is subjoined, that *this engagement to restore Port Egmont,*

cannot,

cannot, nor ought in any wise to affect the question of the prior right of sovereignty of the Malouine otherwise called Falkland's Islands.

THIS conceſſion was accepted by the Earl of Rochford, who declared on the part of his maſter, that the Prince of Maſſeran being authorized by his Catholick Majeſty, *to offer in his Majeſty's name, to the King of Great Britain, a ſatisfaction for the injury done him by diſpoſſeſſing him of Port Egmont*, and having ſigned a declaration expreſſing that his Catholick Majeſty *diſavows the expedition againſt Port Egmont*, and engages to reſtore it in the ſtate in which it ſtood before the 10th of June 1770, *his Britannick majeſty will look upon the ſaid declaration, together with the full performance of the engagement on the part of his Catholick Majeſty, as a ſatisfaction for the injury done to the crown of Great Britain.*

This is all that was originally demanded. The expedition is disavowed, and the island is restored. An injury is acknowledged by the reception of Lord Rochford's paper, who twice mentions the word *injury* and twice the word *satisfaction.*

The Spaniards have stipulated that the grant of possession shall not preclude the question of prior right, a question which we shall probably make no haste to discuss, and a right of which no formal resignation was ever required. This reserve has supplied matter for much clamour, and perhaps the English ministry would have been better pleased had the declaration been without it. But when we have obtained all that was asked, why should we complain that we have not more? When the possession is conceded, where is the evil that the right, which that concession supposes to be merely hypothetical, is referred to the

the Greek Calends for a future disquisition? Were the Switzers less free or less secure, because after their defection from the house of Austria they had never been declared independent before the treaty of Westphalia? Is the King of France less a sovereign because the King of England partakes his title?

If sovereignty implies undisputed right, scarce any prince is a sovereign through his whole dominions; if sovereignty consists in this, that no superiour is acknowledged, our King reigns at Port Egmont with sovereign authority. Almost every new acquired territory is in some degree controvertible, and till the controversy is decided, a term very difficult to be fixed, all that can be had is real possession and actual dominion.

This surely is a sufficient answer to the feudal gabble of a man who is every day lessening that splendour of character which once illuminated the kingdom, then dazzled, and afterwards inflamed it; and for whom it will be happy if the nation shall at last dismiss him to nameless obscurity, with that equipoise of blame and praise which Corneille allows to Richlieu, a man who, I think, had much of his merit, and many of his faults.

Chacun parle a son gré de ce grand Cardinal,
Mais pour moi je n'en dirai rien;
Il m' a fait trop de bien pour en dire du mal,
Il m' a fait trop de mal pour en dire du bien.

To push advantages too far is neither generous nor just. Had we insisted on a concession of antecedent right, it may not misbecome us either as moralists or politicians, to consider what Grimaldi could have answered. We have already, he might say, granted you the whole effect of right, and have not denied you the name. We have not said that the right was ours before this con-

concession, but only that what right we had, is not by this concession vacated. We have now for more than two centuries ruled large tracts of the American continent, by a claim which perhaps is valid only upon this consideration, that no power can produce a better; by the right of discovery and prior settlement. And by such titles almost all the dominions of the earth are holden, except that their original is beyond memory, and greater obscurity gives them greater veneration. Should we allow this plea to be annulled, the whole fabrick of our empire shakes at the foundation. When you suppose yourselves to have first descried the disputed island, you suppose what you can hardly prove. We were at least the general discoverers of the Magellanick region, and have hitherto held it with all its adjacencies. The justice of this tenure the world has hitherto admitted, and yourselves at least tacitly allowed it, when about twenty years ago you desisted from your purposed expedition, and expresly disowned any design of settling, where you are now not content to settle and to reign, without extorting such a confession of original right, as may invite every other nation to follow you.

To considerations such as these, it is reasonable to impute that anxiety of the Spaniards, from which the importance of this island is inferred by Junius, one of the few writers of his despicable faction whose name does not disgrace the page of an opponent. The value of the thing disputed may be very different to him that gains and him that loses it. The Spaniards, by yielding Falkland's island, have admitted a precedent of what they think encroachment; have suffered a breach to be made in the outworks of their empire; and notwithstanding the reserve of prior right, have suffered a dangerous exception to the prescriptive tenure of their American territories.

SUCH is the loss of Spain; let us now compute the profit of Britain. We have, by obtaining a disavowal of Buccarelli's expedition; and a restitution of our settlement, maintained the honour of the crown, and the superiority of our influence. Beyond this what have we acquired? What, but a bleak and gloomy solitude, an island thrown aside from human use, stormy in winter, and barren in summer; an island which not the southern savages have dignified with habitation; where a garrison must be kept in a state that contemplates with envy the exiles of Siberia; of which the expence will be perpetual, and the use only occasional; and which, if fortune smile upon our labours, may become a nest of smugglers in peace, and in war the refuge of future Buccaniers. To all this the Government has now given ample attestation, for the island has been since abandoned, and perhaps was kept only to quiet clamours, with an intention, not then wholly concealed, of quitting it in a short time.

THIS is the country of which we have now possession, and of which a numerous party pretends to wish that we had murdered thousands for the titular sovereignty. To charge any men with such madness, approaches to an accusation defeated by its own incredibility. As they have been long accumulating falsehoods, it is possible that they are now only adding another to the heap, and that they do not mean all that they profess. But of this faction what evil may not be credited? They have hitherto shewn no virtue, and very little wit, beyond that mischievous cunning for which it is held by Hale that children may be hanged.

As war is the last of remedies, *cuncta prius tentanda*, all lawful expedients must be used to avoid it. As war is the extremity of evil, it is surely the duty of those whose station intrusts them with the care of nations, to avert it from their charge.

There

There are diseases of animal nature which nothing but amputation can remove; so there may, by the depravation of human passions, be sometimes a gangrene in collective life for which fire and the sword are the necessary remedies; but in what can skill or caution be better shewn than preventing such dreadful operations, while there is yet room for gentler methods?

It is wonderful with what coolness and indifference the greater part of mankind see war commenced. Those that hear of it at a distance, or read of it in books, but have never presented its evils to their minds, consider it as little more than a splendid game, a proclamation, an army, a battle, and a triumph. Some indeed must perish in the most successful field, but they die upon the bed of honour, *resign their lives amidst the joys of conquest, and, filled with England's glory, smile in death.*

THE

The life of a modern soldier is ill represented by heroick fiction. War has means of destruction more formidable than the cannon and the sword. Of the thousands and ten thousands that perished in our late contests with France and Spain, a very small part ever felt the stroke of an enemy; the rest languished in tents and ships, amidst damps and putrefaction; pale, torpid, spiritless, and helpless; gasping and groaning, unpitied among men, made obdurate by long continuance of hopeless misery; and were at last whelmed in pits, or heaved into the ocean, without notice and without remembrance. By incommodious encampments and unwholesome stations, where courage is useless, and enterprise impracticable, fleets are silently dispeopled, and armies sluggishly melted away.

Thus is a people gradually exhausted, for the most part with little effect. The wars of civilized nations make very slow changes in in the ſyſtem of empire. The public perceives ſcarcely any alteration but an increaſe of debt; and the few individuals who are benefited, are not ſuppoſed to have the cleareſt right to their advantages. If he that ſhared the danger enjoyed the profit, and after bleeding in the battle grew rich by the victory, he might ſhew his gains without envy. But at the concluſion of a ten years war, how are we recompenſed for the death of multitudes and the expence of millions, but by contemplating the ſudden glories of paymaſters and agents, contractors and commiſſaries, whoſe equipages ſhine like meteors, and whoſe palaces riſe like exhalations.

THESE are the men who, without virtue, labour, or hazard, are growing rich as their country is impoveriſhed; they rejoice when obſtinacy or ambition adds another year to ſlaughter and devaſtation; and laugh from their deſks at bravery and ſcience, while they are adding figure to figure,

and

and cipher to cipher; hoping for a new contract from a new armament, and computing the profits of a siege or tempest.

Those who suffer their minds to dwell on these considerations will think it no great crime in the ministry that they have not snatched with eagerness the first opportunity of rushing into the field, when they were able to obtain by quiet negociation all the real good that victory could have brought us.

Of victory indeed every nation is confident before the sword is drawn; and this mutual confidence produces that wantonness of bloodshed that has so often desolated the world. But it is evident, that of contradictory opinions one must be wrong, and the history of mankind does not want examples that may teach caution to the daring, and moderation to the proud.

LET us not think our laurels blaſted by condeſcending to inquire, whether we might not poſſibly grow rather leſs than greater by attacking Spain. Whether we ſhould have to contend with Spain alone, whatever has been promiſed by our patriots, may very reaſonably be doubted. A war declared for the empty ſound of an ancient title to a Magellanick rock would raiſe the indignation of the earth againſt us. Theſe encroachers on the waſte of nature, ſays our ally the Ruſſian, if they ſucceed in their firſt effort of uſurpation, will make war upon us for a title to Kamſchatſcha. Theſe univerſal ſettlers, ſays our ally the Dane, will in a ſhort time ſettle upon Greenland, and a fleet will batter Copenhagen, till we are willing to confeſs that it always was their own.

IN a quarrel like this, it is not poſſible that any power ſhould favour us, and it is very likely that ſome would oppoſe us. The

French,

French, we are told, are otherwiſe employed; the conteſts between the King of France and his own ſubjects are ſufficient to withold him from ſupporting Spain. But who does not know that a foreign war has often put a ſtop to civil diſcords? It withdraws the attention of the publick from domeſtick grievances, and affords opportunities of diſmiſſing the turbulent and reſtleſs to diſtant employments. The Spaniards have always an argument of irreſiſtible perſuaſion. If France will not ſupport them againſt England, they will ſtrengthen England againſt France.

But let us indulge a dream of idle ſpeculation, and ſuppoſe that we are to engage with Spain, and with Spain alone; it is not even yet very certain that much advantage will be gained. Spain is not eaſily vulnerable; her kingdom, by the loſs or ceſſion of many fragments of dominion, is become ſolid and compact. The

Spaniards

Spaniards have indeed no fleet able to oppose us, but they will not endeavour actual opposition; they will shut themselves up in their own territories, and let us exhaust our seamen in a hopeless siege. They will give commissions to privateers of every nation, who will prey upon our merchants without possibility of reprisal. If they think their plate fleet in danger, they will forbid it to set sail, and live a while upon the credit of treasure which all Europe knows to be safe; and which, if our obstinacy should continue till they can no longer be without it, will be conveyed to them with secrecy and security by our natural enemies the French, or by the Dutch our natural allies.

But the whole continent of Spanish America will lie open to invasion; we shall have nothing to do but march into these wealthy regions, and make their present masters confess that they were always ours by ancient right. We ſhall throw braſs and iron out of our houſes, and nothing but ſilver will be ſeen among us.

All this is very deſirable, but it is not certain that it can be eaſily attained. Large tracts of America were added by the laſt war to the Britiſh dominions; but, if the faction credit their own Apollo, they were conquered in Germany. They at beſt are only the barren parts of the continent, the refuſe of the earlier adventurers, which the French, who came laſt, had taken only as better than nothing.

Against the Spaniſh dominions we have never hitherto been able to do much. A few privateers have grown rich at their expence, but no ſcheme of conqueſt has yet been ſucceſsful. They are defended not by walls mounted with cannons which by cannons may be battered, but by the ſtorms of the deep and the vapours of the land, by the flames of calenture and blaſts of peſtilence.

In the reign of Elizabeth, the favourite period of English greatness, no enterprises against America had any other consequence than that of extending English navigation. Here Cavendish perished after all his hazards; and here Drake and Hawkins, great as they were in knowledge and in fame, having promised honour to themselves and dominion to the country, sunk by desperation and misery in dishonourable graves.

During the protectorship of Cromwell, a time of which the patriotick tribes still more ardently desire the return, the Spanish dominions were again attempted; but here, and only here, the fortune of Cromwell made a pause. His forces were driven from Hispaniola, his hopes of possessing the West Indies vanished, and Jamaica was taken, only that the whole expedition might not grow ridiculous.

The attack of Carthagena is yet remembered, where the Spaniards from the ramparts saw their invaders destroyed by the hostility of the elements; poisoned by the air, and crippled by the dews; where every hour swept away battalions; and in the three days that passed between the descent and re-embarkation, half an army perished.

In the last war the Havanna was taken, at what expence is too well remembered. May my country be never cursed with such another conquest!

These instances of miscarriage, and these arguments of difficulty, may perhaps abate the military ardour of the Publick. Upon the opponents of the government their operation will be different; they wish for war, but not for conquest; victory would defeat their purposes equally with peace, because prosperity would naturally continue trust in those hands which had used it fortunately. The patriots gratified themselves

ſelves with expectations that ſome ſiniſtrous accident, or erroneous conduct, might diffuſe diſcontent and inflame malignity. Their hope is malevolence, and their good is evil.

Of their zeal for their country we have already had a ſpecimen. While they were terrifying the nation with doubts whether it was any longer to exiſt; while they repreſented invaſive armies as hovering in the clouds, and hoſtile fleets as emerging from the deeps; they obſtructed our levies of ſeamen, and embarraſſed our endeavours of defence. Of ſuch men he thinks with unneceſſary candour who does not believe them likely to have promoted the miſcarriage which they deſired, by intimidating our troops or betraying our counſels.

It is conſidered as an injury to the Publick by thoſe ſanguinary ſtateſmen, that though the fleet has been refitted and manned, yet no hostilities have followed; and they who sat wishing for misery and slaughter are disappointed of their pleasure. But as peace is the end of war, it is the end likewise of preparations for war; and he may be justly hunted down as the enemy of mankind, that can chuse to snatch by violence and bloodshed, what gentler means can equally obtain.

THE ministry are reproached as not daring to provoke an enemy, lest ill success should discredit and displace them. I hope that they had better reasons; that they paid some regard to equity and humanity; and considered themselves as entrusted with the safety of their fellow-subjects, and as the destroyers of all that should be superfluously slaughtered. But let us suppose that their own safety had some influence on their conduct, they will not, however, sink to a level with their enemies. Though the motive might be selfish, the act was innocent. They who grow rich by administering phyſick, are not to be numbered with them that get money by diſpenſing poiſon. If they maintain power by harmleſſneſs and peace, they muſt for ever be at a great diſtance from ruffians who would gain it by miſchief and confuſion. The watch of a city may guard it for hire; but are well employed in protecting it from thoſe who lie in wait to fire the ſtreets and rob the houſes amidſt the conflagration.

An unſucceſsful war would undoubtedly have had the effect which the enemies of the Miniſtry ſo earneſtly deſire; for who could have ſuſtained the diſgrace of folly ending in misfortune? But had wanton invaſion undeſervedly proſpered, had Falkland's Iſland been yielded unconditionally with every right prior and poſterior; though the rabble might have ſhouted, and the windows have blazed, yet thoſe who know the value of life, and the uncertainty of publick credit, would have mur-

mured, perhaps unheard, at the increase of our debt and the loss of our people.

This thirst of blood, however the visible promoters of sedition may think it convenient to shrink from the accusation, is loudly avowed by Junius, the writer to whom his party owes much of its pride, and some of its popularity. Of Junius it cannot be said, as of Ulysses, that he scatters ambiguous expressions among the vulgar; for he cries *havock* without reserve, and endeavours to let slip the dogs of foreign or of civil war, ignorant whither they are going, and careless what may be their prey.

Junius has sometimes made his satire felt, but let not injudicious admiration mistake the venom of the shaft for the vigour of the bow. He has sometimes sported with lucky malice; but to him that knows his company, it is not hard to be sarcastick in a mask. While he walks like Jack the

Giant-

Giant-killer in a coat of darkneſs, he may do much miſchief with little ſtrength. Novelty captivates the ſuperficial and thoughtleſs; vehemence delights the diſcontented and turbulent. He that contradicts acknowledged truth will always have an audience; he that vilifies eſtabliſhed authority will always find abettors.

JUNIUS burſt into notice with a blaze of impudence which has rarely glared upon the world before, and drew the rabble after him as a monſter makes a ſhow. When he had once provided for his ſafety by impenetrable ſecrecy, he had nothing to combat but truth and juſtice, enemies whom he knows to be feeble in the dark. Being then at liberty to indulge himſelf in all the immunities of inviſibility; out of the reach of danger, he has been bold; out of the reach of ſhame, he has been confident. As a rhetorician, he has had the art of perſuading when he ſeconded deſire; as a reaſoner, he has convinced thoſe who had no

doubt

doubt before; as a moralist, he has taught that virtue may disgrace; and as a patriot, he has gratified the mean by insults on the high. Finding sedition ascendant, he has been able to advance it; finding the nation combustible, he has been able to inflame it. Let us abstract from his wit the vivacity of insolence, and withdraw from his efficacy the sympathetick favour of Plebeian malignity; I do not say that we shall leave him nothing; the cause that I defend scorns the help of falsehood; but if we leave him only his merit, what will be his praise?

It is not by his liveliness of imagery, his pungency of periods, or his fertility of allusion, that he detains the cits of London, and the boors of Middlesex. Of style and sentiment they take no cognizance. They admire him for virtues like their own, for contempt of order and violence of outrage, for rage of defamation and audacity of falsehood. The Supporters of the Bill of Rights

Rights feel no niceties of compoſition, nor dexterities of ſophiſtry; their faculties are better proportioned to the bawl of Bellas, or barbarity of Beckford; but they are told that Junius is on their ſide, and they are therefore ſure that Junius is infallible. Thoſe who know not whither he would lead them, reſolve to follow him; and thoſe who cannot find his meaning, hope he means rebellion.

Junius is an unuſual phænomenon, on which ſome have gazed with wonder and ſome with terrour, but wonder and terrour are tranſitory paſſions. He will ſoon be more cloſely viewed or more attentively examined, and what folly has taken for a comet that from its flaming hair ſhook peſtilence and war, inquiry will find to be only a meteor formed by the vapours of putrefying democracy, and kindled into flame by the effervеſcence of intereſt ſtruggling with conviction; which after having plunged

ged its followers in a bog, will leave us inquiring why we regarded it.

YET though I cannot think the ſtyle of Junius ſecure from criticiſm, though his expreſſions are often trite, and his periods feeble, I ſhould never have ſtationed him where he has placed himſelf, had I not rated him by his morals rather than his faculties. What, ſays Pope, muſt be the prieſt, where a monkey is the God? What muſt be the drudge of a party of which the heads are Wilkes and Croſby, Sawbridge and Townſend?

JUNIUS knows his own meaning and can therefore tell it. He is an enemy to the miniſtry, he ſees them growing hourly ſtronger. He knows that a war at once unjuſt and unſucceſsful would have certainly diſplaced them, and is therefore, in his zeal for his country, angry that war was not unjuſtly made, and unſucceſsfully conducted. But there are others whoſe thoughts

are

are less clearly expressed, and whose schemes perhaps are less consequentially digested; who declare that they do not wish for a rupture, yet condemn the ministry for not doing that, by which a rupture would naturally have been made.

If one party resolves to demand what the other resolves to refuse, the dispute can be determined only by arbitration; and between powers who have no common superiour, there is no other arbitrator than the sword.

Whether the ministry might not equitably have demanded more, is not worth a question. The utmost exertion of right is always invidious, and where claims are not easily determinable is always dangerous. We asked all that was necessary, and persisted in our first claim without mean recession, or wanton aggravation. The Spaniards found us resolute, and complied after a short struggle.

THE real crime of the ministry is, that they have found the means of avoiding their own ruin; but the charge against them is multifarious and confused, as will happen, when malice and discontent are ashamed of their complaint. The past and the future are complicated in the censure. We have heard a tumultuous clamour about honour and rights, injuries and insults, the British flag, and the Favourite's rudder, Buccarelli's conduct, and Grimaldi's declarations, the Manilla ransom, delays and reparation.

THROUGH the whole argument of the faction runs the general errour, that our settlement on Falkland's Island was not only lawful but unquestionable; that our right was not only certain but acknowledged; and that the equity of our conduct was such, that the Spaniards could not blame or obstruct it without combating their own conviction, and opposing the general opinion of mankind.

If once it be discovered that, in the opinion of the Spaniards, our settlement was usurped, our claim arbitrary, and our conduct insolent, all that has happened will appear to follow by a natural concatenation. Doubts will produce disputes and disquisition; disquisition requires delay, and delay causes inconvenience.

Had the Spanish government immediately yielded unconditionally all that was required, we might have been satisfied; but what would Europe have judged of their submission? That they shrunk before us as a conquered people, who having lately yielded to our arms, were now compelled to sacrifice to our pride. The honour of the Publick is indeed of high importance; but we must remember that we have had to transact with a mighty King and a powerful nation, who have unluckily been taught to think that they have honour to keep or lose as well as ourselves.

WHEN the Admiralty were told in June of the warning given to Hunt, they were, I ſuppoſe, informed that Hunt had firſt provoked it by warning away the Spaniards, and naturally conſidered one act of inſolence as balanced by another, without expecting that more would be done on either ſide. Of repreſentations and remonſtrances there would be no end, if they were to be made whenever ſmall commanders are uncivil to each other; nor could peace ever be enjoyed, if upon ſuch tranſient provocations it be imagined neceſſary to prepare for war. We might then, it is ſaid, have increaſed our force with more leiſure and leſs inconvenience; but this is to judge only by the event. We omitted to diſturb the Publick, becauſe we did not ſuppoſe that an armament would be neceſſary.

SOME months afterwards, as has been told, Buccarelli, the governor of Buenos Ayres, ſent againſt the ſettlement of Port

Egmont a force which enſured the conqueſt. The Spaniſh commander required the Engliſh captains to depart, but they thinking that reſiſtance neceſſary which they knew to be uſeleſs, gave the Spaniards the right of preſcribing terms of capitulation. The Spaniards impoſed no new condition except that the ſloop ſhould not ſail under twenty days; and of this they ſecured the performance by taking off the rudder.

To an inhabitant of the land there appears nothing in all this unreaſonable or offenſive. If the Engliſh intended to keep their ſtipulation, how were they injured by the detention of the rudder? If the rudder be to a ſhip what his tail is in fables to a fox, the part in which honour is placed, and of which the violation is never to be endured, I am ſorry that the *Favourite* ſuffered an indignity, but cannot yet think it a cauſe for which nations ſhould ſlaughter one another.

When Buccarelli's invaſion was known, and the dignity of the crown infringed, we demanded reparation and prepared for war, and we gained equal reſpect by the moderation of our terms, and the ſpirit of our exertion. The Spaniſh miniſter immediately denied that Buccarelli had received any particular orders to ſeize Port Egmont, nor pretended that he was juſtified otherwiſe than by the general inſtructions by which the American governors are required to exclude the ſubjects of other powers.

To have inquired whether our ſettlement at Port Egmont was any violation of the Spaniſh rights, had been to enter upon a diſcuſſion which the pertinacity of political diſputants might have continued without end. We therefore called for reſtitution, not as a confeſſion of right, but as a reparation of honour, which required that we ſhould be reſtored to our former ſtate upon the island, and that the King of Spain should disavow the action of his governor.

In return to this demand, the Spaniards expected from us a disavowal of the menaces with which they had been first insulted by Hunt; and if the claim to the island be supposed doubtful, they certainly expected it with equal reason. This, however, was refused, and our superiority of strength gave validity to our arguments.

But we are told that the disavowal of the King of Spain is temporary and fallacious; that Buccarelli's armament had all the appearance of regular forces and a concerted expedition; and that he is not treated at home as a man guilty of piracy, or as disobedient to the orders of his master.

That the expedition was well planned, and the forces properly supplied, affords no proof of communication between the governor and his court. Those who are intrusted with the care of kingdoms in another hemisphere, must always be trusted with power to defend them.

As little can be inferred from his reception at the Spanish court. He is not punished indeed, for what has he done that deserves punishment? He was sent into America to govern and defend the dominions of Spain. He thought the English were encroaching, and drove them away. No Spaniard thinks that he has exceeded his duty, nor does the King of Spain charge him with excess. The boundaries of dominion in that part of the world have not yet been settled; and he mistook, if a mistake there was, like a zealous subject, in his master's favour.

But all this inquiry is superfluous. Considered as a reparation of honour, the disavowal of the King of Spain, made in the

the ſight of all Europe, is of equal value, whether true or falſe. There is indeed no reaſon to queſtion its veracity; they, however, who do not believe it, muſt allow the weight of that influence by which a great prince is reduced to diſown his own commiſſion.

But the general orders upon which the governor is acknowledged to have acted, are neither diſavowed nor explained. Why the Spaniards ſhould diſavow the defence of their own territories, the warmeſt diſputant will find it difficult to tell; and if by an explanation is meant an accurate delineation of the ſouthern empire, and the limitation of their claims beyond the line, it cannot be imputed to any very culpable remiſſneſs, that what has been denied for two centuries to the European powers, was not obtained in a haſty wrangle about a petty ſettlement.

The ministry were too well acquainted with negociation to fill their heads with such idle expectations. The question of right was inexplicable and endless. They left it as it stood. To be restored to actual possession was easily practicable. This restoration they required and obtained.

But they should, say their opponents, have insisted upon more; they should have exacted not only reparation of our honour but repayment of our expence. Nor are they all satisfied with the recovery of the costs and damages of the present contest; they are for taking this opportunity of calling in old debts, and reviving our right to the ransom of Manilla,

The Manilla ransom has, I think, been most mentioned by the inferior bellowers of sedition. Those who lead the faction know that it cannot be remembered much to their advantage. The followers of Lord

Rockingham remember that his miniſtry begun and ended without obtaining it; the adherents to Grenville would be told, that he could never be taught to underſtand our claim. The law of nations made little of his knowledge. Let him not, however, be depreciated in his grave. If he was ſometimes wrong, he was often right.

Of reimburſement the talk has been more confident, though not more reaſonable. The expences of war have been often deſired, have been ſometimes required, but were never paid; or never, but when reſiſtance was hopeleſs, and there remained no choice between ſubmiſſion and deſtruction.

Of our late equipments I know not from whom the charge can be very properly expected. The king of Spain diſavows the violence which provoked us to arm, and for the miſchiefs which he did not do, why should he pay? Buccarelli, though he had learned all the arts of an East-Indian governor, could hardly have collected at Buenos Ayres a sum sufficient to satisfy our demands. If he be honest, he is hardly rich; and if he be disposed to rob, he has the misfortune of being placed where robbers have been before him.

THE king of Spain indeed delayed to comply with our proposals, and our armament was made necessary by unsatisfactory answers and dilatory debates. The delay certainly increased our expences, and it is not unlikely that the increase of our expences put an end to the delay.

BUT this is the inevitable process of human affairs. Negociation requires time. What is not apparent to intuition must be found by inquiry. Claims that have remained doubtful for ages cannot be settled in a day. Reciprocal complaints are not easily

easily adjusted but by reciprocal compliance. The Spaniards thinking themselves entitled to the island, and injured by Captain Hunt, in their turn demanded satisfaction, which was refused; and where is the wonder if their concessions were delayed! They may tell us, that an independent nation is to be influenced not by command, but by persuasion; that if we expect our proposals to be received without deliberation, we assume that sovereignty which they do not grant us; and that if we arm while they are deliberating, we must indulge our martial ardour at our own charge.

The English ministry asked all that was reasonable, and enforced all that they asked. Our national honour is advanced, and our interest, if any interest we have, is sufficiently secured. There can be none amongst us to whom this transaction does not seem happily concluded, but those who having fixed their hopes on public calamities,

mities, ſat like vultures waiting for a day of carnage. Having worn out all the arts of domeſtick ſedition, having wearied violence, and exhauſted falſehood, they yet flattered themſelves with ſome aſſiſtance from the pride or malice of Spain; and when they could no longer make the people complain of grievances which they did not feel, they had the comfort yet of knowing that real evils were poſſible, and their reſolution is well known of charging all evil on their governours.

The reconciliation was therefore conſidered as the loſs of their laſt anchor; and received not only with the fretfulneſs of diſappointment but the rage of deſperation. When they found that all were happy in ſpite of their machinations, and the ſoft effulgence of peace ſhone out upon the nation, they felt no motion but that of ſullen envy; they could not, like Milton's prince of hell, abſtract themſelves a moment from their evil; as they have not

the

the wit of Satan, they have not his virtue; they tried once again what could be done by sophistry without art, and confidence without credit. They represented their Sovereign as dishonoured and their country as betrayed, or, in their fiercer paroxysms of fury, reviled their Sovereign as betraying it.

THEIR pretences I have here endeavoured to expose, by showing that more than has been yielded was not to be expected, that more perhaps was not to be desired, and that if all had been refused, there had scarcely been an adequate reason for a war.

THERE was perhaps never much danger of war or of refusal, but what danger there was, proceeded from the faction. Foreign nations, unacquainted with the insolence of Common Councils, and unaccustomed to the howl of Plebeian patriotism, when they heard of rabbles and riots, of petitions and

remon-

remonſtrances, of diſcontent in Surrey, Derbyſhire, and Yorkſhire, when they ſaw the chain of ſubordination broken, and the legiſlature threatened and defied, naturally imagined that ſuch a government had little leiſure for Falkland's Iſland; they ſuppoſed that the Engliſh when they returned ejected from Port Egmont, would find Wilkes inveſted with the protectorate; or ſee the mayor of London, what the French have formerly ſeen their mayors of the palace, the commander of the army and tutor of the King; that they would be called to tell their tale before the Common Council; and that the world was to expect war or peace from a vote of the ſubſcribers to the Bill of Rights.

But our enemies have now loſt their hopes, and our friends I hope are recovered from their fears. To fancy that our government can be ſubverted by the rabble, whom its lenity has pampered into impudence,

dence, is to fear that a city may be drowned by the overflowing of its kennels. The diſtemper which cowardice or malice thought either decay of the vitals, or reſolution of the nerves, appears at laſt to have been nothing more than a political *phthiriaſis*, a diſeaſe too loathſome for a plainer name; but the effect of negligence rather than of weakneſs, and of which the ſhame is greater than the danger.

Among the diſturbers of our quiet are ſome animals of greater bulk, whom their power of roaring perſuaded us to think formidable, but we now perceive that ſound and force do not always go together. The noiſe of a ſavage proves nothing but his hunger.

After all our broils, foreign and domeſtick, we may at laſt hope to remain awhile in quiet, amuſed with the view of our own ſucceſs. We have gained political ſtrength by the increaſe of our reputation; we have gained real ſtrength by the reparation of our navy; we have ſhewn Europe that ten years of war have not yet exhauſted us; and we have enforced our ſettlement on an iſland on which twenty years ago we durſt not venture to look.

THESE are the gratifications only of honeſt minds; but there is a time in which hope comes to all. From the preſent happineſs of the publick the patriots themſelves may derive advantage. To be harmleſs though by impotence obtains ſome degree of kindneſs; no man hates a worm as he hates a viper; they were once dreaded enough to be deteſted, as ſerpents that could bite; they have now ſhewn that they can only hiſs, and may therefore quietly ſlink into holes, and change their ſlough unmoleſted and forgotten.

March, 1771.

THE

PATRIOT.

Addressed to the

ELECTORS of GREAT BRITAIN.

> They bawl for Freedom in their senseless mood,
> Yet still revolt when Truth would set them free,
> Licence they mean, when they cry Liberty,
> For who loves that must first be wise and good.
>
> Milton.

[1774.]

4)

THE

PATRIOT.

TO improve the golden moment of opportunity, and catch the good that is within our reach, is the great art of life. Many wants are ſuffered, which might once have been ſupplied; and much time is loſt in regretting the time which had been loſt before.

AT the end of every ſeven years comes the Saturnalian ſeaſon, when the freemen of Great Britain may pleaſe themſelves with the choice of their repreſentatives. This happy day has now arrived, ſomewhat ſooner than it could be claimed.

To ſelect and depute thoſe, by whom laws are to be made, and taxes to be granted, is a high dignity and an important truſt: and it is the buſineſs of every elector to conſider, how this dignity may be well ſuſtained, and this truſt faithfully diſcharged.

It ought to be deeply impreſſed on the minds of all who have voices in this national deliberation, that no man can deſerve a ſeat in parliament who is not a Patriot. No other man will protect our rights, no other man can merit our confidence.

A patriot is he whoſe public conduct is regulated by one ſingle motive, the love of his country; who, as an agent in parliament, has for himſelf neither hope nor fear, neither kindneſs nor reſentment, but refers every thing to the common intereſt.

That

THAT of five hundred men, such as this degenerate age affords, a majority can be found thus virtuously abstracted, who will affirm? Yet there is no good in despondence: vigilance and activity often effect more than was expected. Let us take a Patriot where we can meet him; and that we may not flatter ourselves by false appearances, distinguish those marks which are certain, from those which may deceive: for a man may have the external appearance of a Patriot, without the constituent qualities; as false coins have often lustre, tho' they want weight.

SOME claim a place in the list of Patriots by an acrimonious and unremitting opposition to the Court.

THIS mark is by no means infallible. Patriotism is not necessarily included in rebellion. A man may hate his King, yet not love his Country. He that has been refuſed a reaſonable or unreaſonable requeſt, who thinks his merit under-rated, and ſees his influence declining, begins ſoon to talk of natural equality, the abſurdity of *many made for one*, the original compact, the foundation of authority, and the majeſty of the people. As his political melancholy increaſes, he tells, and perhaps dreams of the advances of the prerogative, and the dangers of arbitrary power; yet his deſign in all his declamation is not to benefit his country, but to gratify his malice.

THESE, however, are the moſt honeſt of the opponents of government; their patriotiſm is a ſpecies of diſeaſe; and they feel ſome part of what they expreſs. But the greater, far the greater number of thoſe who rave and rail, and inquire and accuſe, neither ſuſpect nor fear, nor care for the Public; but hope to force their way to riches by virulence and invective,

and

and are vehement and clamorous, only that they may be ſooner hired to be ſilent.

A MAN ſometimes ſtarts up a Patriot, only by diſſeminating diſcontent and propagating reports of ſecret influence, of dangerous counſels, of violated rights and encroaching uſurpation.

THIS practice is no certain note of Patriotiſm. To inſtigate the populace with rage beyond the provocation, is to ſuſpend public happineſs, if not to deſtroy it. He is no lover of his country, that unneceſſarily diſturbs its peace. Few errors, and few faults of government can juſtify an appeal to the rabble; who ought not to judge of what they cannot underſtand, and whoſe opinions are not propagated by reaſon, but caught by contagion.

THE fallaciouſneſs of this note of patriotiſm is particularly apparent, when the clamour continues after the evil is paſt. They who are ſtill filling our ears with Mr. Wilkes, and the Frecholderes of Middleſex, lament a grievance, that is now at an end. Mr. Wilkes may be choſen, if any will chooſe him, and the precedent of his excluſion makes not any honeſt, or any decent man, think himſelf in danger.

It may be doubted whether the name of a Patriot can be fairly given as the reward of ſecret ſatire, or open outrage. To fill the news-papers with ſly hints of corruption and intrigue, to circulate the Middleſex Journal and London Pacquet, may indeed be zeal; but it may likewiſe be intereſt and malice. To offer a petition, not expected to be granted; to inſult a King with a rude remonſtrance, only becauſe there is no puniſhment for legal inſolence, is not courage, for there is no danger; nor patriotiſm, for it tends the ſubverſion of order, and lets wickedneſs looſe upon the land, by deſtroying the reverence due to ſovereign authority.

It is the quality of Patriotiſm to be jealous and watchful, to obſerve all ſecret machinations, and to ſee public dangers at a diſtance. The true *Lover of his country* is ready to communicate his fears and to ſound the alarm, whenever he perceives the approach of miſchief. But he ſounds no alarm, when there is no enemy: he never terrifies his countrymen till he is terrified himſelf. The patriotiſm therefore may be juſtly doubted of him, who profeſſes to be diſturbed by incredibilities; who tells, that the laſt peace was obtained by bribing the Princeſs of Wales; that the King is graſping at arbitrary power; and that becauſe the French in the new conqueſts enjoy their own laws, there is a deſign at court of aboliſhing in England the trial by juries.

STILL less does the true Patriot circulate opinions which he knows to be false. No man, who loves his country, fills the nation with clamorous complaints, that the Protestant religion is in danger, because *Popery is established in the extensive province of Quebec*, a falsehood so open and shameless, that it can need no confutation among those who know that of which it is almost impossible for the most unenlightened zealot to be ignorant,

THAT Quebec is on the other side of the Atlantic, at too great a distance to do much good or harm to the European world:

THAT the inhabitants, being French, were always Papists, who are certainly more dangerous as enemies, than as subjects:

THAT though the province be wide, the people are few, probably not so many

as

as may be found in one of the larger English counties:

THAT persecution is not more virtuous in a Protestant than a Papist; and that while we blame Lewis the Fourteenth, for his dragoons and his gallies, we ought, when power comes into our hands, to use it with greater equity:

THAT when Canada with its inhabitants was yielded, the free enjoyment of their religion was stipulated; a condition, of which King William, who was no propagator of Popery, gave an example nearer home, at the surrender of Limerick:

THAT in an age, where every mouth is open for *liberty of conscience*, it is equitable to shew some regard to the conscience of a Papist, who may be supposed, like other men, to think himself safest in his own religion; and that those at least, who enjoy

enjoy a toleration, ought not to deny it to our new ſubjects.

If liberty of conſcience be a natural right, we have no power to with-hold it; if it be an indulgence, it may be allowed to Papiſts, while it is not denied to other ſects.

A patriot is neceſſarily and invariably a lover of the people. But even this mark may ſometimes deceive us.

The people is a very heterogeneous and confuſed maſs of the wealthy and the poor, the wiſe and the fooliſh, the good and the bad. Before we confer on a man, who careſſes the people, the title of Patriot, we muſt examine to what part of the people he directs his notice. It is proverbially ſaid, that he who diſſembles his own character, may be known by that of his companions. If the

the candidate of Patriotiſm endeavours to infuſe right opinions into the higher ranks, and by their influence to regulate the lower; if he conſorts chiefly with the wiſe, the temperate, the regular, and the virtuous, his love of the people may be rational and honeſt. But if his firſt or principal application be to the indigent, who are always inflammable; to the weak, who are naturally ſuſpicious; to the ignorant, who are eaſily miſled; and to the profligate, who have no hope but from miſchief and confuſion; let his love of the people be no longer boaſted. No man can reaſonably be thought a lover of his country, for roaſting an ox, or burning a boot, or attending the meeting at Mile-End, or regiſtering his name in the Lumber-Troop. He may, among the drunkards be a *hearty fellow*, and among ſober handicraftſmen, a *free-ſpoken gentleman*; but he muſt have ſome better diſtinction before he is a *Patriot.*

A PATRIOT is always ready to countenance the juſt claims, and animate the reaſonable hopes of the people; he reminds them frequently of their rights, and ſtimulates them to reſent encroachments, and to multiply ſecurities.

BUT all this may be done in appearance, without real patriotiſm. He that raiſes falſe hopes to ſerve a preſent purpoſe, only makes a way for diſappointment and diſcontent. He who promiſes to endeavour, what he knows his endeavours unable to effect, means only to delude his followers by an empty clamour of ineffectual zeal.

A TRUE Patriot is no laviſh promiſer: he undertakes not to ſhorten parliaments; to repeal laws; or to change the mode of repreſentation, tranſmitted by our anceſtors: he knows that futurity is not in his power, and that all times are not alike favourable to change.

Much lefs does he make a vague and indefinite promife of obeying the mandates of his conftituents. He knows the prejudices of faction, and the inconftancy of the multitude. He would firft inquire, how the opinion of his conftituents fhall be taken. Popular inftructions are commonly the work, not of the wife and fteady, but the violent and rafh; meetings held for directing reprefentatives are feldom attended but by the idle and the diffolute; and he is not without fufpicion, that of his conftituents, as of other numbers of men, the fmaller part may often be the wifer.

He confiders himfelf as deputed to promote the publick good, and to preferve his conftituents, with the reft of his countrymen, not only from being hurt by others, but from hurting themfelves.

The common marks of patriotifm having been examined, and fhewn to be fuch as artifice may counterfeit, or folly misapply, it cannot be improper to consider, whether there are not some characteristical modes of speaking or acting, which may prove a man to be NOT A PATRIOT.

In this inquiry, perhaps clearer evidence may be discovered, and firmer persuasion attained; for it is commonly easier to know what is wrong than what is right; to find what we should avoid, than what we should pursue.

As war is one of the heaviest of national evils, a calamity, in which every species of misery is involved; as it sets the general safety to hazard, suspends commerce, and desolates the country; as it exposes great numbers to hardships, dangers, captivity, and death; no man, who desires the publick prosperity, will inflame general resentment by aggravating minute injuries, or or enforcing diſputable rights of little importance.

It may therefore be ſafely pronounced, that thoſe men are no Patriots, who when the national honour was vindicated in the ſight of Europe, and the Spaniards having invaded what they call their own, had ſhrunk to a diſavowal of their attempt and a relaxation of their claim, would ſtill have [redacted] inſtigated us to a war for a bleak and barren ſpot in the Magellanic ocean, of which no uſe could be made unleſs it were a place of exile for the hypocrites of patriotiſm.

Yet let it not be forgotten, that by the howling violence of patriotic rage, the nation was for a time exaſperated to ſuch madneſs, that for a barren rock, under a ſtormy ſky, we might have now been fighting and dying, had not our competi-

tors

tors been wiser than ourselves; and those who are now courting the favour of the people by noisy professions of public spirit, would, while they were counting the profits of their artifice, have enjoyed the patriotic pleasure of hearing sometimes, that thousands had been slaughtered in a battle, and sometimes that a navy had been dispeopled by poisoned air and corrupted food.

HE that wishes to see his country robbed of its rights, cannot be a Patriot.

THAT man therefore is no Patriot, who justifies the ridiculous claims of American usurpation; who endeavours to deprive the nation of its natural and lawful authority over its own colonies; those colonies, which were settled under English protection; were constituted by an English charter; and have been defended by English arms.

To suppose, that by sending out a colony, the nation established an independent power; that

that when, by indulgence and favour, emigrants are become rich, they ſhall not contribute to their own defence, but at their own pleaſure; and that they ſhall not be included, like millions of their fellow-ſubjects, in the general ſyſtem of repreſentation; involves ſuch an accumulation of abſurdity, as nothing but the ſhew of patriotiſm could palliate.

He that accepts protection, ſtipulates obedience. We have always protected the Americans; we may therefore ſubject them to government.

The leſs is included in the greater. That power which can take away life, may ſeize upon property. The parliament may enact for America a law of capital puniſhment; it may therefore eſtabliſh a mode and proportion of taxation.

But there are ſome who lament the ſtate of the poor Boſtonians, becauſe they cannot all be ſuppoſed to have committed acts of rebellion, yet all are involved in the penalty impoſed. This, they ſay, is to violate the firſt rule of juſtice, by condemning the innocent to ſuffer with the guilty.

THIS deſerves ſome notice, as it ſeems dictated by equity and humanity, however it may raiſe contempt, by the ignorance which it betrays of the ſtate of man, and the ſyſtem of things. That the innocent ſhould be confounded with the guilty, is undoubtedly an evil; but it is an evil which no care or caution can prevent. National crimes require national puniſhments, of which many muſt neceſſarily have their part, who have not incurred them by perſonal guilt. If rebels ſhould fortify a town, the cannon of lawful authority will endanger equally the harmleſs burghers and the criminal garriſon.

In some cases, those suffer most who are least intended to be hurt. If the French in the late war had taken an English city, and permitted the natives to keep their dwellings, how could it have been recovered, but by the slaughter of our friends? A bomb might as well destroy an Englishman as a Frenchman; and by famine we know that the inhabitants would be the first that should perish.

This infliction of promiscuous evil may therefore be lamented, but cannot be blamed. The power of lawful government must be maintained; and the miseries which rebellion produces, can be charged only on the rebels.

That man likewise is *not a Patriot*, who denies his governors their due praise, and who conceals from the people the benefits which they receive. Those therefore can lay no claim to this illustrious appellation, who impute want of public ſpirit to the late parliament; an aſſembly of men, whom, notwithſtanding ſome fluctuation of counſel, and ſome weakneſs of agency, the nation muſt always remember with gratitude, ſince it is indebted to them for a very ample conceſſion in the reſignation of protections, and a wiſe and honeſt attempt to improve the conſtitution, in the new judicature inſtituted for the trial of elections.

The right of protection, which might be neceſſary when it was firſt claimed, and was very conſiſtent with that liberality of immunities in which the feudal conſtitution delighted, was by its nature liable to abuſe, and had in reality been ſometimes miſapplied, to the evaſion of the law and the defeat of juſtice. The evil was perhaps not adequate to the clamour; nor is it very certain, that the poſſible good of this privilege was not more than equal to the poſſible evil. It is however plain, that whether they gave any thing or not to the Public, they at least lost something from themselves. They divested their dignity of a very splendid distinction, and shewed that they were more willing than their predecessors to stand on a level with their fellow subjects.

The new mode of trying elections, if it be found effectual, will diffuse its consequences further than seems yet to be foreseen. It is, I believe, generally considered as advantageous only to those who claim seats in parliament; but, if to chuse representatives be one of the most valuable rights of Englishmen, every voter must consider that law as adding to his happiness, which makes his suffrage efficacious; since it was vain to chuse, while the election could be controlled by any other power.

With what imperious contempt of ancient rights, and what audaciousness of arbitrary authority, former parliaments have judged the diſputes about elections, it is not neceſſary to relate. The claim of a candidate, and the right of electors are ſaid ſcarcely to have been, even in appearance, referred to conſcience; but to have been decided by party, by paſſion, by prejudice, or by frolic. To have friends in the borough was of little uſe to him, who wanted friends in the houſe; a pretence was eaſily found to evade a majority, and the ſeat was at laſt his, that was choſen not by his electors, but his fellow-ſenators.

Thus the nation was inſulted with a mock election, and the parliament was filled with ſpurious repreſentatives; one of the moſt important claims, that of a right to ſit in the ſupreme council of the kingdom, was debated in jeſt, and no man could be confident of ſucceſs from the juſtice of his cauſe.

A DISPUTED

A DISPUTED election is now tried with the same scrupulousness and solemnity, as any other title. The candidate that has deserved well of his neighbours, may now be certain of enjoying the effect of their approbation; and the elector, who has voted honestly for known merit, may be certain that he has not voted in vain.

SUCH was the parliament, which some of those, who are now aspiring to sit in another, have taught the rabble to consider as an unlawful convention of men, worthless, venal, and prostitute, slaves of the court, and tyrants of the people.

THAT the next House of Commons may act upon the principles of the last, with more constancy and higher spirit, must be the wish of all who wish well to the Publick; and it is surely not too much to expect, that the nation will recover from its delusion, and unite in a general abhorrence of those who, by deceiving the credulous with fictitious mischiefs, overbearing the weak by audacity of falsehood, by appealing to the judgment of ignorance, and flattering the vanity of meanness, by slandering honesty and insulting dignity, have gathered round them whatever the kingdom can supply of base, and gross, and profligate; and *raised by merit to this bad eminence*, arrogate to themselves the name of PATRIOTS.

Taxation no Tyranny;

AN

ANSWER

TO THE

RESOLUTIONS AND ADDRESS

OF THE

AMERICAN CONGRESS.

[1775.]

A brilliant & correct composition, [illegible] lished March 1775 in which [illegible] Mr [illegible] handles the weapons of reason, irony & ridicule against the American Congress with admirable address.

TAXATION

NO TYRANNY

IN all the parts of human knowledge, whether terminating in science merely speculative, or operating upon life private or civil, are admitted some fundamental principles, or common axioms, which being generally received are little doubted, and being little doubted have been rarely proved.

Of these axioms and acknowledged truths, it is the fate of some to become less evident by endeavours to explain them, however necessary such endeavours may be made by the misapprehensions of absurdity, or the sophistries of interest. It is difficult to prove the principles of science because

TAXATION

NO TYRANNY.

IN all the parts of human knowledge, whether terminating in ſcience merely ſpeculative, or operating upon life private or civil, are admitted ſome fundamental principles, or common axioms, which being generally received are little doubted, and being little doubted have been rarely proved.

OF theſe gratuitous and acknowledged truths it is often the fate to become leſs evident by endeavours to explain them, however neceſſary ſuch endeavours may be made by the miſapprehenſions of abſurdity, or the ſophiſtries of intereſt. It is difficult to prove the principles of ſcience, becauſe

because notions cannot always be found more intelligible than those which are questioned. It is difficult to prove the principles of practice, because they have for the most part not been discovered by investigation, but obtruded by experience, and the demonstrator will find, after an operose deduction, that he has been trying to make that seen which can be only felt.

Of this kind is the position, that *the supreme power of every community has the right of requiring from all its subjects such contributions as are necessary to the public safety or public prosperity*, which was considered by all mankind as comprising the primary and essential condition of all political society, till it became disputed by those zealots of anarchy, who have denied to the Parliament of Britain the right of taxing the American Colonies.

In favour of this exemption of the Americans from the authority of their

lawful

lawful ſovereign, and the dominion of their mother-country, very loud clamours have been raiſed, and many wild aſſertions advanced, which by ſuch as borrow their opinions from the reigning faſhion have been admitted as arguments; and what is ſtrange, though their tendency is to leſſen Engliſh honour, and Engliſh power, have been heard by Engliſh-men with a wiſh to find them true. Paſſion has in its firſt violence controlled intereſt, as the eddy for a while runs againſt the ſtream.

To be prejudiced is always to be weak; yet there are prejudices ſo near to laudable, that they have been often praiſed, and are always pardoned. To love their country has been conſidered as virtue in men, whoſe love could not be otherwiſe than blind, becauſe their preference was made without a compariſon; but it has never been my fortune to find, either in ancient or modern writers, any honourable mention of thoſe,

those, who have with equal blindness hated their country.

THESE antipatriotic prejudices are the abortions of Folly impregnated by Faction, which being produced against the standing order of Nature, have not strength sufficient for long life. They are born only to scream and perish, and leave those to contempt or detestation, whose kindness was employed to nurse them into mischief.

To perplex the opinion of the Publick many artifices have been used, which, as usually happens when falsehood is to be maintained by fraud, lose their force by counteracting one another.

THE nation is sometimes to be mollified by a tender tale of men, who fled from tyranny to rocks and deserts, and is persuaded to lose all claims of justice, and all sense of dignity, in compassion for a harmleſs people, who having worked hard for bread in a wild country, and obtained by the ſlow progreſſion of manual induſtry the accommodations of life, are now invaded by unprecedented oppreſſion, and plundered of their properties by the harpies of taxation.

We are told how their induſtry is obſtructed by unnatural reſtraints, and their trade confined by rigorous prohibitions; how they are forbidden to enjoy the products of their own ſoil, to manufacture the materials which Nature ſpreads before them, or to carry their own goods to the neareſt market: and ſurely the generoſity of Engliſh virtue will never heap new weight upon thoſe that are already overladen, will never delight in that dominion, which cannot be exerciſed but by cruelty and outrage.

But while we are melting in ſilent ſorrow, and in the tranſports of delirious

pity

pity dropping both the ſword and balance from our hands, another friend of the Americans thinks it better to awaken another paſſion, and tries to alarm our intereſt, or excite our veneration, by accounts of their greatneſs and their opulence, of the fertility of their land, and the ſplendour of their towns. We then begin to conſider the queſtion with more evenneſs of mind, are ready to conclude that thoſe reſtrictions are not very oppreſſive which have been found conſiſtent with this ſpeedy growth of proſperity, and begin to think it reaſonable that they, who thus flouriſh under the protection of our government, ſhould contribute ſomething towards its expence.

But we are ſoon told that the Americans, however wealthy, cannot be taxed; that they are the deſcendants of men who left all for liberty, and that they have conſtantly preſerved the principles and ſtub-

bornneſs

bornness of their progenitors; that they are too obſtinate for perſuaſion, and too powerful for conſtraint; that they will laugh at argument, and defeat violence; that the continent of North America contains three millions, not of men merely, but of Whigs, of Whigs fierce for liberty, and diſdainful of dominion; that they multiply with the fecundity of their own rattle-ſnakes, ſo that every quarter of a century doubles their numbers.

MEN accuſtomed to think themſelves maſters do not love to be threatened. This talk is, I hope, commonly thrown away, or raiſes paſſions different from thoſe which it was intended to excite. Inſtead of terrifying the Engliſh hearer to tame acquieſcence, it diſpoſes him to haſten the experiment of bending obſtinacy before it is become yet more obdurate, and convinces him that it is neceſſary to attack a nation thus prolific while we may yet hope to prevail. When he is told through what extent of territory we must travel to subdue them, he recollects how far, a few years ago, we travelled in their defence. When it is urged that they will shoot up like the Hydra, he naturally considers how the Hydra was destroyed.

NOTHING dejects a trader like the interruption of his profits. A commercial people, however magnanimous, shrinks at the thought of declining traffick, and an unfavourable balance. The effect of this terrour has been tried. We have been stunned with the importance of our American commerce, and heard of merchants with warehouses that are never to be emptied, and of manufacturers starving for want of work.

THAT our commerce with America is profitable, however less than ostentatious or deceitful estimates have made it, and that

it

it is our intereſt to preſerve it, has never been denied; but ſurely it will moſt effectually be preſerved, by being kept always in our own power. Conceſſions may promote it for a moment, but ſuperiority only can enſure its continuance. There will always be a part, and always a very large part of every community that have no care but for themſelves, and whoſe care for themſelves reaches little farther than impatience of immediate pain, and eagerneſs for the neareſt good. The blind are ſaid to feel with peculiar nicety. They who look but little into futurity, have perhaps the quickeſt ſenſation of the preſent. A merchant's deſire is not of glory, but of gain; not of publick wealth, but of private emolument; he is therefore rarely to be conſulted about war and peace, or any deſigns of wide extent and diſtant conſequence.

Yet this, like other general characters, will ſometimes fail. The traders of *Birmingham* have reſcued themſelves from all imputation of narrow ſelfiſhneſs by a manly recommendation to Parliament of the rights and dignity of their native country.

To theſe men I do not intend to aſcribe an abſurd and enthuſiaſtick contempt of intereſt, but to give them the rational and juſt praiſe of diſtinguiſhing real from ſeeming good, of being able to ſee through the cloud of interpoſing difficulties, to the laſting and ſolid happineſs of victory and ſettlement.

Lest all theſe topicks of perſuaſion ſhould fail, the great actor of patriotiſm has tried another, in which terrour and pity are happily combined, not without a proper ſuperaddition of that admiration which latter ages have brought into the

drama.

drama. The heroes of Boſton he tells us, if the ſtamp act had not been repealed, would have left their town, their port, and their trade, have reſigned the ſplendour of opulence, and quitted the delights of neighbourhood, to diſperſe themſelves over the country, where they would till the ground, and fiſh in the rivers, and range the mountains, AND BE FREE.

THESE ſurely are brave words. If the mere ſound of freedom can operate thus powerfully, let no man hereafter doubt the ſtory of the Pied Piper. *The removal of the people of Boſton into the country*, ſeems even to the congreſs not only *difficult in its execution*, but *important in its conſequences*. The difficulty of execution is beſt known to the Boſtonians themſelves; the conſequence, alas! will only be, that they will leave good houſes to wiſer men.

Yet before they quit the comforts of a warm home for the founding something which they think better, he cannot be thought their enemy who advises them to consider well whether they shall find it. By turning fishermen or hunters, woodmen or shepherds they may become wild, but it is not so easy to conceive them free; for who can be more a slave than he that is driven by force from the comforts of life, is compelled to leave his house to a casual comer, and whatever he does, or wherever he wanders, finds every moment some new testimony of his own subjection? If choice of evil be freedom, the felon in the gallies has his option of labour or of stripes. The Bostonian may quit his house to starve in the fields; his dog may refuse to set, and smart under the lash, and they may then congratulate each other upon the smiles of liberty, *profuse of bliss, and pregnant with delight.*

To treat ſuch deſigns as ſerious, would be to think too contemptuouſly of Boſtonian underſtandings. The artifice indeed is not new: the bluſterer who threatened in vain to deſtroy his opponent, has ſometimes obtained his end, by making it believe that he would hang himſelf.

But terrours and pity are not the only means by which the taxation of the Americans is oppoſed. There are thoſe who profeſs to uſe them only as auxiliaries to reaſon and juſtice, who tell us, that to tax the Colonies is uſurpation and oppreſſion, an invaſion of natural and legal rights, and a violation of thoſe principles which ſupport the conſtitution of Engliſh government.

This queſtion is of great importance. That the Americans are able to bear taxation is indubitable; that their refuſal may be over-ruled is highly probable: but power is no sufficient evidence of truth. Let us examine our own claim, and the objections of the recusants, with caution proportioned to the event of the decision, which must convict one part of robbery, or the other of rebellion.

A TAX is a payment exacted by authority from part of the community for the benefit of the whole. From whom, and in what proportion such payment shall be required, and to what uses it shall be applied, those only are to judge to whom government is intrusted. In the British dominion taxes are apportioned, levied, and appropriated by the states assembled in parliament.

OF every empire all the subordinate communities are liable to taxation, because they all share the benefits of government, and therefore ought all to furnish their proportion of the expence.

THIS the Americans have never openly denied. That it is their duty to pay the coſt of their own ſafety they ſeem to admit; nor do they refuſe their contribution to the exigencies, whatever they may be, of the Britiſh empire; but they make this participation of the public burden a duty of very uncertain extent, and imperfect obligation, a duty temporary, occaſional, and elective, of which they reſerve to themſelves the right of ſettling the degree, the time, and the duration, of judging when it may be required, and when it has been performed.

THEY allow to the ſupreme power nothing more than the liberty of notifying to them its demands or its neceſſities. Of this notification they profeſs to think for themſelves, how far it ſhall influence their counſels, and of the neceſſities alleged, how far they ſhall endeavour to relieve them. They aſſume the excluſive power of ſettling not only the mode, but the

quantity

quantity of this payment. They are ready to co-operate with all the other dominions of the king; but they will co-operate by no means which they do not like, and at no greater charge than they are willing to bear.

THIS claim, wild as it may ſeem, this claim, which ſuppoſes dominion without authority, and ſubjects without ſubordination, has found among the libertines of policy many clamorous and hardy vindicators. The laws of Nature, the rights of humanity, the faith of charters, the danger of liberty, the encroachments of uſurpation, have been thundered in our ears, ſometimes by intereſted faction, and ſometimes by honeſt ſtupidity.

IT is ſaid by Fontenelle, that if twenty philoſophers ſhall reſolutely deny that the preſence of the ſun makes the day, he will not deſpair but whole nations may adopt the

the opinion. So many political dogmatists have denied to the Mother-country the power of taxing the Colonies, and have enforced their denial with so much violence of outcry, that their sect is already very numerous, and the publick voice suspends its decision.

In moral and political questions the contest between interest and justice has been often tedious and often fierce, but perhaps it never happened before, that justice found much opposition with interest on her side.

For the satisfaction of this inquiry, it is necessary to consider how a Colony is constituted, what are the terms of migration as dictated by Nature, or settled by compact, and what social or political rights the man loses, or acquires, that leaves his country to establish himself in a distant plantation.

Of two modes of migration the hiſtory of mankind informs us, and ſo far as I can yet diſcover, of two only.

In countries where life was yet unadjuſted, and policy unformed, it ſometimes happened that by the diſſenſions of heads of families, by the ambition of daring adventurers, by ſome accidental preſſure of diſtreſs, or by the mere diſcontent of idleneſs, one part of the community broke off from the reſt, and numbers, greater or ſmaller, forſook their habitations, put themſelves under the command of ſome favourite of fortune, and with or without the conſent of their countrymen or governours, went out to ſee what better regions they could occupy, and in what place, by conqueſt or by treaty, they could gain a habitation.

Sons of enterpriſe like theſe, who committed to their own ſwords their hopes and their lives, when they left their country, became another nation, with designs and prospects, and interests, of their own. They looked back no more to their former home; they expected no help from those whom they had left behind; if they conquered, they conquered for themselves; if they were destroyed, they were not by any other power either lamented or revenged.

Of this kind seem to have been all the migrations of the early world, whether historical or fabulous, and of this kind were the eruptions of those nations which from the North invaded the Roman empire, and filled Europe with new sovereignties.

But when, by the gradual admission of wiser laws and gentler manners, society became more compacted and better regulated, it was found that the power of every

every people consisted in union, produced by one common interest, and operating in joint efforts and consistent councils.

FROM this time Independence perceptibly wasted away. No part of the nation was permitted to act for itself. All now had the same enemies and the same friends; the Government protected individuals, and individuals were required to refer their designs to the prosperity of the Government.

BY this principle it is, that states are formed and consolidated. Every man is taught to consider his own happiness as combined with the public prosperity, and to think himself great and powerful, in proportion to the greatness and power of his Governors.

HAD the Western continent been discovered between the fourth and tenth century, when all the Northern world was in motion;

tion; and had navigation been at that time sufficiently advanced to make so long a passage easily practicable, there is little reason for doubting but the intumescence of nations would have found its vent, like all other expansive violence, where there was least resistance; and that Huns and Vandals, instead of fighting their way to the South of Europe, would have gone by thousands and by myriads under their several chiefs to take possession of regions smiling with pleasure and waving with fertility, from which the naked inhabitants were unable to repel them.

EVERY expedition would in those days of laxity have produced a distinct and independent state. The Scandinavian heroes might have divided the country among them, and have spread the feudal subdivision of regality from Hudson's Bay to the Pacific Ocean.

BUT

But Columbus came five or six hundred years too late for the candidates of sovereignty. When he formed his project of discovery, the fluctuations of military turbulence had subsided, and Europe began to regain a settled form, by established government and regular subordination. No man could any longer erect himself into a chieftain, and lead out his fellow-subjects by his own authority to plunder or to war. He that committed any act of hostility by land or sea, without the commission of some acknowledged sovereign, was considered by all mankind as a robber or a pirate, names which were now of little credit, and of which therefore no man was ambitious.

Columbus in a remoter time would have found his way to some discontented Lord, or some younger brother of a petty Sovereign, who would have taken fire at his proposal, and have quickly kindled

with

with equal heat a troop of followers; they would have built ſhips, or have ſeized them, and have wandered with him at all adventures as far as they could keep hope in their company. But the age being now paſt of vagrant excurſion and fortuitous hoſtility, he was under the neceſſity of travelling from court to court, ſcorned and repulſed as a wild projector, an idle promiſer of kingdoms in the clouds: nor has any part of the world yet had reaſon to rejoice that he found at laſt reception and employment.

In the ſame year, in a year hitherto diſaſtrous to mankind, by the Portugueſe was diſcovered the paſſage of the Indies, and by the Spaniards the coaſt of America. The nations of Europe were fired with boundleſs expectation, and the diſcoverers purſuing their enterpriſe, made conqueſts in both hemiſpheres of wide extent. But the adventurers were contented with plunder;

though they took gold and silver to themselves, they seized islands and kingdoms in the name of their Sovereigns. When a new region was gained, a governour was appointed by that power which had given the commission to the conqueror; nor have I met with any European but Stukeley of London, that formed a design of exalting himself in the newly found countries to independent dominion.

To secure a conquest, it was always necessary to plant a colony, and territories thus occupied and settled were rightly considered as mere extensions or processes of empire; as ramifications which by the circulation of one publick interest communicated with the original source of dominion, and which were kept flourishing and spreading by the radical vigour of the Mother-country.

The Colonies of England differ no otherwise from those of other nations, than as the

the Engliſh conſtitution differs from theirs. All Government is ultimately and eſſentially abſolute, but ſubordinate ſocieties may have more immunities, or individuals greater liberty, as the operations of Government are differently conducted. An Engliſhman in the common courſe of life and action feels no reſtraint. An Engliſh Colony has very liberal powers of regulating its own manners and adjuſting its own affairs. But an Engliſh individual may by the ſupreme authority be deprived of liberty, and a Colony diveſted of its powers, for reaſons of which that authority is the only judge.

In ſovereignty there are no gradations. There may be limited royalty, there may be limited conſulſhip; but there can be no limited government. There muſt in every ſociety be ſome power or other from which there is no appeal, which admits no reſtrictions, which pervades the whole maſs of the community, regulates and adjuſts all ſubordination, enacts laws or repeals them, erects or annuls judicatures, extends or contracts privileges, exempt itſelf from queſtion or control, and bounded only by phyſical neceſſity.

By this power, wherever it ſubſiſts, all legiſlation and juriſdiction is animated and maintained. From this all legal rights are emanations, which, whether equitably or not, may be legally recalled. It is not infallible, for it may do wrong; but it is irreſiſtible, for it can be reſiſted only by rebellion, by an act which makes it queſtionable what ſhall be thenceforward the ſupreme power.

An Engliſh Colony is a number of perſons, to whom the King grants a Charter permitting them to ſettle in ſome diſtant country, and enabling them to conſtitute a Corporation, enjoying ſuch powers as the Charter grants, to be adminiſtered in ſuch forms as the Charter preſcribes. As a

Corporation

Corporation they make laws for themselves, but as a Corporation subsisting by a grant from higher authority, to the control of that authority they continue subject.

As men are placed at a greater distance from the Supreme Council of the kingdom, they must be intrusted with ampler liberty of regulating their conduct by their own wisdom. As they are more secluded from easy recourse to national judicature, they must be more extensively commissioned to pass judgment on each other,

For this reason our more important and opulent Colonies see the appearance and feel the effect of a regular Legislature, which in some places has acted so long with unquestioned authority, that it has forgotten whence that authority was originally derived.

To their Charters the Colonies owe, like other corporations, their political exiſtence. The ſolemnities of legiſlation, the adminiſtration of juſtice, the ſecurity of property, are all beſtowed upon them by the royal grant. Without their Charter there would be no power among them, by which any law could be made, or duties enjoined, any debt recovered, or criminal puniſhed.

A CHARTER is a grant of certain powers or privileges given to a part of the community for the advantage of the whole, and is therefore liable by its nature to change or to revocation. Every act of Government aims at publick good. A Charter, which experience has ſhewn to be detrimental to the nation, is to be repealed; becauſe general proſperity muſt always be preferred to particular intereſt. If a Charter be uſed to evil purpoſes, it is forfeited, as the weapon is taken away which is injuriouſly employed.

THE

THE Charter therefore by which provincial governments are constituted, may be always legally, and where it is either inconvenient in its nature, or misapplied in its use, may be equitably repealed; by such repeal the whole fabrick of subordination is immediately destroyed, and the constitution sunk at once into a chaos: the society is dissolved into a tumult of individuals, without authority to command, or obligation to obey; without any punishment of wrongs but by personal resentment, or any protection of right but by the hand of the possessor.

A COLONY is to the Mother-country as a member to the body, deriving its action and its strength from the general principle of vitality; receiving from the body, and communicating to it, all the benefits and evils of health and disease; liable in dangerous maladies to sharp applications, of which the body however must partake the

 pain;

pain; and exposed, if incurably tainted, to amputation, by which the body likewise will be mutilated.

The Mother-country always considers the Colonies thus connected, as parts of itself; the prosperity or unhappiness of either is the prosperity or unhappiness of both; not perhaps of both in the same degree, for the body may subsist, though less commodiously, without a limb, but the limb must perish if it be parted from the body.

Our Colonies therefore, however distant, have been hitherto treated as constituent parts of the British Empire: The inhabitants incorporated by English Charters, are entitled to all the rights of Englishmen. They are governed by English laws, entitled to English dignities, regulated by English counsels, and protected by English arms; and it seems to follow by consequence

ſequence not eaſily avoided, that they are ſubject to Engliſh government, and chargeable by Engliſh taxation.

To him that conſiders the nature, the original, the progreſs, and the conſtitution of the Colonies, who remembers that the firſt diſcoverers had commiſſions from the Crown, that the firſt ſettlers owe to a Charter their civil forms and regular magiſtracy, and that all perſonal immunities and legal ſecurities, by which the condition of the ſubject has been from time to time improved, have been excended to the Coloniſts, it will not be doubted but the Parliament of England has a right to bind them by ſtatutes, and *to bind them in all caſes whatſoever*, and has therefore a natural and conſtitutional power of laying upon them any tax or impoſt, whether external or internal, upon the product of land, or the manufactures of induſtry, in the exigencies of war, or in the time

of

of profound peace, for the defence of America, *for the purpose of raising a revenue*, or for any other end beneficial to the Empire.

THERE are some, and those not inconsiderable for number, nor contemptible for knowledge, who except the power of taxation from the general dominion of Parliament, and hold, that whatever degrees of obedience may be exacted, or whatever authority may be exercised in other acts of Government, there is still reverence to be paid to money, and that legislation passes its limits when it violates the purse.

OF this exception, which by a head not fully impregnated with politicks is not easily comprehended, it is alleged as an unanswerable reason, that the Colonies send no representatives to the House of Commons.

IT

It is, ſay the American advocates, the natural diſtinction of a freeman, and the legal privilege of an Engliſhman, that he is able to call his poſſeſſions his own, that he can ſit ſecure in the enjoyment of inheritance or acquiſition, that his houſe is fortified by the law, and that nothing can be taken from him but by his own conſent. This conſent is given for every man by his repreſentative in parliament. The Americans unrepreſented cannot conſent to Engliſh taxations, as a corporation, and they will not conſent as individuals.

Of this argument, it has been obſerved by more than one, that its force extends equally to all other laws, for a freeman is not to be expoſed to puniſhment, or be called to any onerous ſervice but by his own conſent. The Congreſs has extracted a poſition from the fanciful *Monteſquieu*, that *in a free ſtate every man being a free agent ought to be concerned in his own go-*

vernment. Whatever is true of taxation is true of every other law, that he who is bound by it, without his conſent, is not free, for he is not concerned in his own government.

He that denies the Engliſh Parliament the right of taxation, denies it likewiſe the right of making any other laws civil or criminal, yet this power over the Colonies was never yet diſputed by themſelves. They have always admitted ſtatutes for the puniſhment of offences, and for the redreſs or prevention of inconveniencies, and the reception of any law draws after it by a chain which cannot be broken, the unwelcome neceſſity of ſubmitting to taxation.

That a free man is governed by himſelf, or by laws to which he has conſented, is a poſition of mighty ſound: but every man that utters it, with whatever confidence, and every man that hears it, with

whatever

whatever acquiescence, if consent be supposed to imply the power of refusal, feels it to be false. We virtually and implicitly allow the institutions of any Government of which we enjoy the benefit, and solicit the protection. In wide extended dominions, though power has been diffused with the most even hand, yet a very small part of the people are either primarily or secondarily consulted in Legislation. The business of the Publick must be done by delegation. The choice of delegates is made by a select number, and those who are not electors stand idle and helpless spectators of the commonweal, *wholly unconcerned in the government of themselves.*

OF Electors the hap is but little better. They are often far from unanimity in their choice, and where the numbers approach to equality, almost half must be governed not only without, but against their choice.

How

How any man can have consented to institutions established in distant ages, it will be difficult to explain. In the most favourite residence of liberty, the consent of individuals is merely passive, a tacit admission in every community of the terms which that community grants and requires. As all are born the subjects of some state or other, we may be said to have been all born consenting to some system of Government. Other consent than this, the condition of civil life does not allow. It is the unmeaning clamour of the pedants of policy, the delirious dream of republican fanaticism.

BUT hear, ye sons and daughters of liberty, the sounds which the winds are wafting from the Western Continent. The Americans are telling one another, what, if we may judge from their noisy triumph, they have but lately discovered, and what yet is a very important truth: *That they*

are

are entitled to Life, Liberty, and Property, and that they have never ceded to any sovereign power whatever a right to dispose of either without their consent.

While this resolution stands alone, the Americans are free from singularity of opinion; their wit has not yet betrayed them to heresy. While they speak as the naked sons of Nature, they claim but what is claimed by other men, and have withheld nothing but what all with-hold. They are here upon firm ground, behind entrenchments which never can be forced.

Humanity is very uniform. The Americans have this resemblance to Europeans, that they do not always know when they are well. They soon quit the fortress that could neither have been mined by sophistry, nor battered by declamation. Their next resolution declares, that *their ancestors, who first settled the*

Colo-

Colonies, were, at the time of their emigration from the Mother-country, entitled to all the rights, liberties, and immunities of free and natural-born subjects within the realm of England.

THIS likewife is true; but when this is granted, their boaft of original rights is at an end; they are no longer in a State of Nature. Thefe lords of themfelves, thefe kings of *Me*, thefe demigods of independence, fink down to Colonifts, governed by a Charter. If their anceftors were fubjects, they acknowledged a Sovereign; if they had a right to Englifh privileges, they were accountable to Englifh laws, and what muft grieve the Lover of Liberty to difcover, had ceded to the King and Parliament, whether the right or not, at leaft the power of difpofing, *without their confent, of their lives, liberties, and properties.* It therefore is required of them to prove, that the Parliament ever ceded to them a difpenfation from that obedience, which they owe as natural-born ſubjects, or any degree of independence or immunity not enjoyed by other Engliſhmen.

THEY ſay, That by ſuch emigration they by no means forfeited, ſurrendered, or loſt any of thoſe rights; but that *they were, and their deſcendants now are, entitled to the exerciſe and enjoyment of all ſuch of them as their local and other circumſtances enable them to exerciſe and enjoy.*

THAT they who form a ſettlement by a lawful Charter having committed no crime forfeit no privileges, will be readily confeſſed; but what they do not forfeit by any judicial ſentence, they may loſe by natural effects. As man can be but in one place at once, he cannot have the advantages of multiplied reſidence. He that will enjoy the brightneſs of ſunſhine, muſt quit the coolneſs of the ſhade. He who goes voluntarily to America, cannot complain of loſing what he leaves in Europe. He perhaps had a right to vote for a knight or burgess; by crossing the Atlantick he has not nullified his right; but he has made its exertion no longer possible*. By his own choice he has left a country where he had a vote and little property, for another, where he has great property, but no vote. But as this preference was deliberate and unconstrained, he is still *concerned in the government of himself*; he has reduced himself from a voter to one of the innumerable multitude that have no vote. He has truly *ceded his right*, but he still is governed by his own consent; because he has consented to throw his atom of interest into the general mass of the community. Of the consequences of his own act he has no cause to complain; he has chosen, or intended to chuse, the greater good; he is represented, as himself desired, in the general representation.

* Of this reasoning, I owe part to a conversation with Sir John Hawkins.

But the privileges of an American ſcorn the limits of place; they are part of himſelf, and cannot be loſt by departure from his country; they float in the air, or glide under the ocean.

Doris amara ſuam non intermiſceat undam.

A planter, wherever he ſettles, is not only a freeman, but a legiſlator, *ubi imperator, ibi Roma. As the Engliſh Coloniſts are not repreſented in the Britiſh Parliament, they are entitled to a free and excluſive power of legiſlation in their ſeveral legiſlatures, in all caſes of Taxation and internal polity, ſubject only to the negative of the Sovereign, in ſuch manner as has been heretofore uſed and accuſtomed. We cheerfully conſent to the operation of ſuch acts of the Britiſh Parliament as are* bona fide *reſtrained to the regulation of our external commerce—excluding every idea of Taxation, internal or external, for raiſing a revenue on the ſubjects of America without their conſent.*

Their reaſon for this claim is, *that the foundation of Engliſh Liberty, and of all Government, is a right in the People to participate in their Legiſlative Council.*

They inherit, they ſay, *from their anceſtors, the right which their anceſtors poſſeſſed, of enjoying all the privileges of Engliſhmen.* That they inherit the right of their anceſtors is allowed; but they can inherit no more. Their anceſtors left a country where the repreſentatives of the people were elected by men particularly qualified, and where thoſe who wanted qualifications, or who did not uſe them, were bound by the deciſions of men, whom they had not deputed.

The coloniſts are the deſcendants of men, who either had no vote in elections, or who voluntarily reſigned them for ſomething,

thing, in their opinion, of more eſtimation: they have therefore exactly what their anceſtors left them, not a vote in making laws, or in conſtituting legiſlators, but the happineſs of being protected by law, and the duty of obeying it.

WHAT their anceſtors did not carry with them, neither they nor their deſcendants have ſince acquired. They have not, by abandoning their part in one legiſlature, obtained the power of conſtituting another, excluſive and independent, any more than the multitudes, who are now debarred from voting, have a right to erect a ſeparate Parliament for themſelves.

MEN are wrong for want of ſenſe, but they are wrong by halves for want of ſpirit. Since the Americans have diſcovered that they can make a Parliament, whence comes it that they do not think themſelves equally empowered to make a King? If they are ſubjects, whoſe government is conſtituted by a Charter, they can form no body of independent legiſlature. If their rights are inherent and underived, they may by their own ſuffrages encircle with a diadem the brows of Mr. Cuſhing.

It is farther declared by the Congreſs of Philadelphia, *that his Majeſty's Colonies are entitled to all the privileges and immunities granted and confirmed to them by Royal Charters, or ſecured to them by their ſeveral codes of provincial laws.*

The firſt clauſe of this reſolution is eaſily underſtood, and will be readily admitted. To all the privileges which a Charter can convey, they are by a Royal Charter evidently entitled. The ſecond clauſe is of greater difficulty; for how can a provincial law ſecure privileges or immunities to a province?

province? Provincial laws may grant to certain individuals of the province the enjoyment of gainful, or an immunity from onerous offices; they may operate upon the people to whom they relate; but no province can confer provincial privileges on itself. They may have a right to all which the King has given them; but it is a conceit of the other hemisphere, that men have a right to all which they have given to themselves.

A CORPORATION is considered in law as an individual, and can no more extend its own immunities, than a man can by his own choice assume dignities or titles.

THE Legislature of a Colony, let not the comparison be too much disdained, is only the vestry of a larger parish, which may lay a cess on the inhabitants, and enforce the payment; but can extend no influence beyond its own district, must modify its particular regulations by the general law, and whatever may be its internal expences, is ſtill liable to Taxes laid by ſuperior authority.

The Charters given to different provinces are different, and no general right can be extracted from them. The Charter of Pennſylvania, where this Congreſs of anarchy has been impudently held, contains a clauſe admitting in expreſs terms Taxation by the Parliament. If in the other Charters no ſuch reſerve is made, it muſt have been omitted as not neceſſary, becauſe it is implied in the nature of ſubordinate government. They who are ſubject to laws, are liable to Taxes. If any ſuch immunity had been granted, it is ſtill revocable by the Legiſlature, and ought to be revoked, as contrary to the publick good, which is in every Charter ultimately intended.

SUPPOSE it true, that any ſuch exemption is contained in the Charter of Maryland, it can be pleaded only by the Marylanders. It is of no uſe for any other province, and with regard even to them, muſt have been conſidered as one of the grants in which the King has been deceived, and annulled as miſchievous to the Publick, by ſacrificing to one little ſettlement the general intereſt of the Empire; as infringing the ſyſtem of dominion, and violating the compact of Government. But Dr. Tucker has ſhewn that even this Charter promiſes no exemption from Parliamentary Taxes.

IN the controverſy agitated about the beginning of this century, whether the Engliſh laws could bind Ireland, Davenant, who defended againſt Molyneux the claims of England, conſidered it as neceſſary to prove nothing more, than that the preſent Iriſh muſt be deemed a Colony.

THE

THE neceſſary connexion of repreſentatives with Taxes, ſeems to have ſunk deep into many of thoſe minds, that admit ſounds without their meaning.

OUR nation is repreſented in Parliament by an aſſembly as numerous as can well conſiſt with order and diſpatch, choſen by perſons ſo differently qualified in different places, that the mode of choice ſeems to be, for the moſt part, formed by chance, and ſettled by cuſtom. Of individuals far the greater part have no vote, and of the voters few have any perſonal knowledge of him to whom they intruſt their liberty and fortune.

YET this repreſentation has the whole effect expected or deſired; that of ſpreading ſo wide the care of general intereſt, and the participation of publick counſels, that the advantage or corruption of particular men can ſeldom operate with much injury to the Publick.

FOR

For this reason many populous and opulent towns neither enjoy nor desire particular representatives: they are included in the general scheme of publick administration, and cannot suffer but with the rest of the Empire.

It is urged that the Americans have not the same security, and that a British Legislator may wanton with their property; yet if it be true, that their wealth is our wealth, and that their ruin will be our ruin, the Parliament has the same interest in attending to them, as to any other part of the nation. The reason why we place any confidence in our representatives is, that they must share in the good or evil which their counsels shall produce. Their share is indeed commonly consequential and remote; but it is not often possible that any immediate advantage can be extended to such numbers as may prevail against it. We are therefore as secure against

against intentional depravations of Government as human wiſdom can make us, and upon this ſecurity the Americans may venture to repoſe.

It is ſaid by the *Old Member* who has written an *Appeal* againſt the Tax, that *as the produce of American labour is ſpent in Britiſh manufactures, the balance of trade is greatly againſt them; whatever you take directly in Taxes, is in effect taken from your own commerce. If the miniſter ſeizes the money with which the American ſhould pay his debts and come to market, the merchant cannot expect him as a cuſtomer, nor can the debts already contracted be paid.—Suppoſe we obtain from America a million inſtead of one hundred thouſand pounds, it would be ſupplying one perſonal exigence by the future ruin of our commerce.*

Part of this is true; but the *Old Member* ſeems not to perceive, that if his brethren of the Legiſlature know this as well

as

as himſelf, the Americans are in no danger of oppreſſion, ſince by men commonly provident they muſt be ſo taxed, as that we may not loſe one way what we gain another.

THE ſame *Old Member* has diſcovered, that the judges formerly thought it illegal to tax Ireland, and declares that no caſes can be more alike than thoſe of Ireland and America; yet the judges whom he quotes have mentioned a difference. Ireland, they ſay, *hath a Parliament of its own*. When any Colony has an independent Parliament acknowledged by the Parliament of Britain, the caſes will differ leſs. Yet by the 6 Geo. I. chap. 5. the Acts of the Britiſh Parliament bind Ireland.

IT is urged that when Wales, Durham, and Cheſter were diveſted of their particular privileges or ancient government, and reduced

reduced to the ſtate of Engliſh counties, they had repreſentatives aſſigned them.

To thoſe from whom ſomething had been taken, ſomething in return might properly be given. To the Americans their Charters are left as they were, nor have they loſt any thing except that of which their ſedition has deprived them. If they were to be repreſented in Parliament, ſomething would be granted, though nothing is withdrawn.

THE inhabitants of Cheſter, Durham, and Wales, were invited to exchange their peculiar inſtitutions for the power of voting, which they wanted before. The Americans have voluntarily reſigned the power of voting, to live in diſtant and ſeparate governments, and what they have voluntarily quitted, they have no right to claim.

IT

It must always be remembered that they are represented by the same virtual representation as the greater part of Englishmen; and that if by change of place they have less share in the Legislature than is proportionate to their opulence, they by their removal gained that opulence, and had originally and have now their choice of a vote at home, or riches at a distance.

We are told, what appears to the *Old Member* and to others a position that must drive us into inextricable absurdity, that we have either no right, or the sole right of taxing the Colonies. The meaning is, that if we can tax them, they cannot tax themselves; and that if they can tax themselves, we cannot tax them. We answer with very little hesitation, that for the general use of the Empire we have the sole right of taxing them. If they have contributed any thing in their own assemblies, what they contributed was not

paid,

paid, but given; it was not a tax or tribute, but a preſent. Yet they have the natural and legal power of levying money on themſelves for provincial purpoſes, of providing for their own expence, at their own diſcretion. Let not this be thought new or ſtrange; it is the ſtate of every pariſh in the kingdom.

The friends of the Americans are of different opinions. Some think that being unrepreſented they ought to tax themſelves, and others that they ought to have repreſentatives in the Britiſh Parliament.

If they are to tax themſelves, what power is to remain in the ſupreme Legiſlature? That they muſt ſettle their own mode of levying their money is ſuppoſed. May the Britiſh Parliament tell them how much they ſhall contribute? If the ſum may be preſcribed, they will return few thanks for the power of raiſing it; if they are

at

at liberty to grant or to deny, they are no longer subjects.

If they are to be represented, what number of these western orators are to be admitted? This I suppose the parliament must settle; yet if men have a natural and unalienable right to be represented, who shall determine the number of their delegates? Let us however suppose them to send twenty-three, half as many as the kingdom of Scotland, what will this representation avail them? To pay taxes will be still a grievance. The love of money will not be lessened, nor the power of getting it increased.

Whither will this necessity of representation drive us? Is every petty settlement to be out of the reach of government, till it has sent a senator to Parliament; or may two of them or a greater number be forced to unite in a single deputation? What at last is the difference,

ence between him that is taxed by compulſion without repreſentation, and him that is repreſented by compulſion in order to be taxed?

For many reigns the Houſe of Commons was in a ſtate of fluctuation: new burgeſſes were added from time to time, without any reaſon now to be diſcovered; but the number has been fixed for more than a century and a half, and the king's power of increaſing it has been queſtioned. It will hardly be thought fit to new-model the conſtitution in favour of the planters, who, as they grow rich, may buy eſtates in England, and without any innovation, effectually repreſent their native colonies.

The friends of the Americans indeed aſk for them what they do not aſk for themſelves. This ineſtimable right of repreſentation they have never ſolicited. They

They mean not to exchange ſolid money for ſuch airy honour. They ſay, and ſay willingly, that they cannot conveniently be repreſented; becauſe their inference is, that they cannot be taxed. They are too remote to ſhare the general government, and therefore claim the privilege of governing themſelves.

Of the principles contained in the reſolutions of the Congreſs, however wild, indefinite, and obſcure, ſuch has been the influence upon American underſtanding, that from New-England to South-Carolina there is formed a general combination of all the Provinces againſt their Mother-country. The madneſs of independence has ſpread from Colony to Colony, till order is loſt and government deſpiſed, and all is filled with miſrule, uproar, violence, and confuſion. To be quiet is diſaffection, to be loyal is treaſon.

The Congreſs of Philadelphia, an aſſembly convened by its own authority, has promulgated a declaration, in compliance with which the communication between Britain and the greateſt part of North America is now ſuſpended. They ceaſed to admit the importation of Engliſh goods in December 1774, and determine to permit the exportation of their own no longer than to November 1775.

This might ſeem enough, but they have done more. They have declared, that they ſhall treat all as enemies who do not concur with them in diſaffection and perverſeneſs, and that they will trade with none that ſhall trade with Britain.

They threaten to ſtigmatize in their Gazette thoſe who ſhall conſume the products or merchandiſe of their Mother-country, and are now ſearching ſuſpected houſes for prohibited goods.

These

These hoſtile declarations they profeſs themſelves ready to maintain by force. They have armed the militia of their provinces, and ſeized the publick ſtores of ammunition. They are therefore no longer ſubjects, ſince they refuſe the laws of their Sovereign, and in defence of that refuſal are making open preparations for war.

Being now in their own opinion free ſtates, they are not only raiſing armies, but forming alliances, not only haſtening to rebel themſelves, but ſeducing their neighbours to rebellion. They have publiſhed an addreſs to the inhabitants of Quebec, in which diſcontent and reſiſtance are openly incited, and with very reſpectful mention of *the ſagacity of Frenchmen*, invite them to ſend deputies to the Congreſs of Philadelphia, to that ſeat of Virtue and Veracity, whence the people of England are told, that to eſtabliſh popery, *a religion fraught with ſanguinary and impious tenets*, even in Quebec, a country of which the inhabitants are papists, is so contrary to the constitution that it cannot be lawfully done by the legislature itself; where it is made one of the articles of their association, to deprive the conquered French of their religious establishment; and whence the French of Quebec are, at the same time, flattered into sedition, by professions of expecting *from the liberality of sentiment, distinguishing* their *nation*, that *difference of religion will not prejudice them against a hearty amity*, because *the transcendent nature of freedom elevates all who unite in the cause above such low-minded infirmities.*

QUEBEC, however, is at a great distance. They have aimed a stroke from which they may hope for greater and more speedy mischief. They have tried to infect the people of England with the contagion of disloyalty. Their credit is happily not such as gives them influence

proportionate

proportionate to their malice. When they talk of their pretended immunities *guarantied by the plighted faith of Government, and the most solemn compacts with English Sovereigns*, we think ourselves at liberty to inquire when the faith was plighted and the compact made; and when we can only find that King James and King Charles the First promised the settlers in Massachuset's Bay, now famous by the appellation of Bostonians, exemption from taxes for seven years, we infer with Mr. Mauduit, that by this *solemn compact*, they were, after expiration of the stipulated term, liable to taxation.

When they apply to our compassion, by telling us, that they are to be carried from their own country to be tried for certain offences, we are not so ready to pity them, as to advise them not to offend. While they are innocent they are safe.

When they tell of laws made expresly for their punishment, we answer, that tumults and sedition were always punishable, and that the new law prescribes only the mode of execution.

When it is said that the whole town of Boston is distressed for a misdemeanour of a few, we wonder at their shamefulness; for we know that the town of Boston, and all the associated provinces, are now in rebellion to defend or justify the criminals.

If frauds in the imposts of Boston are tried by commission without a jury, they are tried here in the same mode; and why should the Bostonians expect from us more tenderness for them than for ourselves?

If they are condemned unheard, it is because there is no need of a trial. The crime is manifest and notorious. All trial

is

is the investigation of something doubtful. An Italian philosopher observes, that no man desires to hear what he has already seen.

If their assemblies have been suddenly dissolved, what was the reason? Their deliberations were indecent, and their intentions seditious. The power of dissolution is granted and reserved for such times of turbulence. Their best friends have been lately soliciting the King to dissolve his Parliament, to do what they so loudly complain of suffering.

That the same vengeance involves the innocent and guilty is an evil to be lamented, but human caution cannot prevent it, nor human power always redress it. To bring misery on those who have not deserved it, is part of the aggregated guilt of rebellion.

That

That governours have been ſometimes given them only that a great man might get eaſe from importunity, and that they have had judges not always of the deepeſt learning, or the pureſt integrity, we have no great reaſon to doubt, becauſe ſuch misfortunes happen to ourſelves. Whoever is governed will ſometimes be governed ill, even when he is moſt *concerned in his own government.*

That improper officers or magiſtrates are ſent, is the crime or folly of thoſe that ſent them. When incapacity is diſcovered, it ought to be removed; if corruption is detected, it ought to be puniſhed. No government could ſubſiſt for a day, if ſingle errors could juſtify defection.

One of their complaints is not ſuch as can claim much commiſeration from the ſofteſt boſom. They tell us, that we have changed our conduct, and that a tax is

now

now laid by Parliament on thoſe which were never taxed by Parliament before. To this we think it may be eaſily anſwered, that the longer they have been ſpared, the better they can pay.

It is certainly not much their intereſt to repreſent innovation as criminal or invidious; for they have introduced into the hiſtory of mankind a new mode of diſaffection, and have given, I believe, the firſt example of a proſcription publiſhed by a Colony againſt the Mother-country.

To what is urged of new powers granted to the Courts of Admiralty, or the extenſion of authority conferred on the judges, it may be anſwered in a few words, that they have themſelves made ſuch regulations neceſſary; that they are eſtabliſhed for the prevention of greater evils; at the ſame time, it muſt be obſerved,

ſerved, that theſe powers have not been extended ſince the rebellion in America.

One mode of perſuaſion their ingenuity has ſuggeſted, which it may perhaps be leſs eaſy to reſiſt. That we may not look with indifference on the American conteſt, or imagine that the ſtruggle is for a claim, which, however decided, is of ſmall importance and remote conſequence, the Philadelphian Congreſs has taken care to inform us, that they are reſiſting the demands of Parliament, as well for our ſakes as their own.

Their keenneſs of perſpicacity has enabled them to purſue conſequences to a great diſtance; to ſee through clouds impervious to the dimneſs of European ſight; and to find, I know not how, that when they are taxed, we ſhall be enſlaved.

That ſlavery is a miſerable ſtate we have been often told, and doubtleſs many a

Briton

Briton will tremble to find it so near as in America; but how it will be brought hither, the Congress must inform us. The question might distress a common understanding; but the statesmen of the other hemisphere can easily resolve it. Our ministers, they say, are our enemies, and *if they should carry the point of taxation, may with the same army enslave us. It may be said, we will not pay them; but remember*, say the western sages, *the taxes from America, and we may add the men, and particularly the Roman Catholics of this vast continent will then be in the power of your enemies. Nor have you any reason to expect, that after making slaves of us, many of us will refuse to assist in reducing you to the same abject state.*

These are dreadful menaces; but suspecting that they have not much the sound of probability, the Congress proceeds: *Do not treat this as chimerical. Know that in less than half a century the quit-rents reserved*

reſerved to the crown from the numberleſs grants of this vaſt continent will pour large ſtreams of wealth into the royal coffers. If to this be added the power of taxing America at pleaſure, the crown will poſſeſs more treaſure than may be neceſſary to purchaſe the remains *of liberty in your iſland.*

ALL this is very dreadful; but amidſt the terror that ſhakes my frame, I cannot forbear to wiſh that ſome ſluice were opened for theſe ſtreams of treaſure. I ſhould gladly ſee America return half of what England has expended in her defence; and of the ſtream that will *flow ſo largely in leſs than half a century.* I hope a ſmall rill at leaſt may be found to quench the thirſt of the preſent generation, which ſeems to think itſelf in more danger of wanting money than of loſing liberty.

IT is difficult to judge with what intention ſuch airy burſts of malevolence

are

are vented: if ſuch writers hope to deceive, let us rather repel them with ſcorn, than refute them by diſputation.

In this laſt terrifick paragraph are two poſitions that, if our fears do not overpower our reflection, may enable us to ſupport life a little longer. We are told by theſe croakers of calamity, not only that our preſent miniſters deſign to enſlave us, but that the ſame malignity of purpoſe is to deſcend through all their ſucceſſors, and that the wealth to be poured into England by the Pactolus of America will, whenever it comes, be employed to purchaſe *the remains of liberty.*

Of thoſe who now conduct the national affairs we may, without much arrogance, preſume to know more than themſelves, and of thoſe who ſhall ſucceed them, whether miniſter or king, not to know leſs.

The other poſition is, that the *Crown*, if this laudable oppoſition ſhould not be ſucceſsful, *will have the power of taxing America at pleaſure.* Surely they think rather too meanly of our apprehenſions, when they ſuppoſe us not to know what they well know themſelves, that they are taxed, like all other Britiſh ſubjects, by Parliament; and that the Crown has not by the new impoſts, whether right or wrong, obtained any additional power over their poſſeſſions.

It were a curious, but an idle ſpeculation to inquire, what effect theſe dictators of ſedition expect from the diſperſion of their letter among us. If they believe their own complaints of hardſhip, and really dread the danger which they deſcribe, they will naturally hope to communicate the ſame perceptions to their fellow-ſubjects. But probably in America, as in other places, the chiefs are incendiaries, that hope to rob in the tumults of a conflagration, and toſs brands among a rabble paſſively combuſtible. Thoſe who wrote the Addreſs, though they have ſhown no great extent or profundity of mind, are yet probably wiſer than to believe it: but they have been taught by ſome maſter of miſchief, how to put in motion the engine of political electricity; to attract by the ſounds of Liberty and Property, to repel by thoſe of Popery and Slavery; and to give the great ſtroke by the name of Boſton.

When ſubordinate communities oppoſe the decrees of the general legiſlature with defiance thus audacious, and malignity thus acrimonious, nothing remains but to conquer or to yield; to allow their claim of independence, or to reduce them by force to ſubmiſſion and allegiance.

It might be hoped, that no Engliſhman could be found, whom the menaces of our own Coloniſts, juſt reſcued from the French, would not move to indignation, like that of the Scythians, who, returning from war, found themſelves excluded from their own houſes by their ſlaves.

THAT corporations conſtituted by favour, and exiſting by ſufferance, ſhould dare to prohibit commerce with their native country, and threaten individuals by infamy, and ſocieties with at leaſt ſuſpenſion of amity, for daring to be more obedient to government than themſelves, is a degree of inſolence, which not only deſerves to be puniſhed, but of which the puniſhment is loudly demanded by the order of life, and the peace of nations.

YET there have riſen up, in the face of the publick, men who, by whatever corruptions or whatever infatuation, have undertaken to defend the Americans, endeavour

deavour to ſhelter them from reſentment, and propoſe reconciliation without ſubmiſſion.

As political diſeaſes are naturally contagious, let it be ſuppoſed for a moment that Cornwall, ſeized with the Philadelphian frenzy, may reſolve to ſeparate itſelf from the general ſyſtem of the Engliſh conſtitution, and judge of its own rights in its own parliament. A Congreſs might then meet at Truro, and addreſs the other counties in a ſtyle not unlike the language of the American patriots.

"Friends and Fellow-ſubjects,

"We the delegates of the ſeveral towns and pariſhes of Cornwall, aſſembled to deliberate upon our own ſtate and that of our conſtituents, having, after ſerious debate and calm conſideration, ſettled the ſcheme of our future conduct, hold it necessary to declare the resolutions which we think ourselves entitled to form by the unalienable rights of reasonable Beings, and into which we have been compelled by grievances and oppressions, long endured by us in patient silence, not because we did not feel, or could not remove them, but because we were unwilling to give disturbance to a settled government, and hoped that others would in time find like ourselves their true interest and their original powers, and all co-operate to universal happiness.

"But since having long indulged the pleasing expectation, we find general discontent not likely to increase, or not likely to end in general defection, we resolve to erect alone the standard of liberty.

"*Know then*, that you are no longer to consider Cornwall as an English county, visited by English judges, receiving law from

from an English Parliament, or included in any general taxation of the kingdom; but as a state distinct, and independent, governed by its own institutions, administered by its own magistrates, and exempt from any tax or tribute but such as we shall impose upon ourselves.

"WE are the acknowledged descendants of the earliest inhabitants of Britain; of men, who before the time of history took possession of the island desolate and waste, and therefore open to the first occupants. Of this descent, our language is a sufficient proof, which, not quite a century ago, was different from yours.

"SUCH are the Cornishmen; but who are you? who but the unauthorised and lawless children of intruders, invaders, and oppressors? who but the transmitters of wrong, the inheritors of robbery? In claiming independence we claim but little. We might require you to depart from a land which you possess by usurpation, and to restore all that you have taken from us.

"INDEPENDENCE is the gift of Nature. No man is born the master of another. Every Cornishman is a freeman, for we have never resigned the rights of humanity; and he only can be thought free, who is not governed but by his own consent.

"You may urge that the present system of government has descended through many ages, and that we have a larger part in the representation of the kingdom, than any other county.

"ALL this is true, but it is neither cogent nor persuasive. We look to the original of things. Our union with the English counties was either compelled by force, or settled by compact.

"THAT

"THAT which was made by violence, may by violence be broken. If we were treated as a conquered people, our rights might be obſcured, but could never be extinguiſhed. The ſword can give nothing but power, which a ſharper ſword can take away.

"IF our union was by compact, whom could the compact bind but thoſe that concurred in the ſtipulations? We gave our anceſtors no commiſſion to ſettle the terms of future exiſtence. They might be cowards that were frighted, or blockheads that were cheated; but whatever they were, they could contract only for themſelves. What they could eſtabliſh, we can annul.

"AGAINST our preſent form of government it ſhall ſtand in the place of all argument, that we do not like it. While we are governed as we do not like, where is our liberty? We do not like taxes, we will therefore not be taxed, we do not like your laws, and will not obey them.

"THE taxes laid by our repreſentatives are laid, you tell us, by our own conſent: but we will no longer conſent to be repreſented. Our number of legiſlators was originally a burden, and ought to have been refuſed: it is now conſidered as a diſproportionate advantage; who then will complain we reſign it?

"WE ſhall form a Senate of our own, under a Preſident whom the King ſhall nominate, but whoſe authority we will limit, by adjuſting his ſalary to his merit. We will not with-hold a proper ſhare of contribution to the neceſſary expence of lawful government, but we will decide for ourſelves what ſhare is proper, what expence

expence is neceſſary, and what government is lawful.

"Till our counſel is proclaimed independent and unaccountable, we will, after the tenth day of September, keep our Tin in our own hands: you can be ſupplied from no other place, and muſt therefore comply or be poiſoned with the copper of your own kitchens.

"If any Corniſhman ſhall refuſe his name to this juſt and laudable aſſociation, he ſhall be tumbled from St. Michael's Mount, or buried alive in a tin-mine; and if any emiſſary ſhall be found ſeducing Corniſhmen to their former ſtate, he ſhall be ſmeared with tar, and rolled in feathers, and chaſed with dogs out of our dominions.

"From the Corniſh Congreſs at Truro."

Of this memorial what could be ſaid but that it was written in jeſt, or written by by a madman? Yet I know not whether the warmeſt admirers of Pennſylvanian eloquence can find any argument in the Addreſſes of the Congreſs, that is not with greater ſtrength urged by the Corniſhman.

THE argument of the irregular troops of controverſy, ſtripped of its colours, and turned out naked to the view, is no more than this. Liberty is the birthright of man, and where obedience is compelled, there is no Liberty. The anſwer is equally ſimple. Government is neceſſary to man, and where obedience is not compelled, there is no government.

IF the ſubject refuſes to obey, it is the duty of authority to uſe compulſion. Society cannot ſubſiſt but by the power, firſt of making laws, and then of enforcing them.

To one of the threats hiſſed out by the Congreſs, I have put nothing ſimilar into the

the Cornish proclamation; because it is too wild for folly and too foolish for madness. If we do not withhold our King and his Parliament from taxing them, they will cross the Atlantick and enslave us.

How they will come they have not told us; perhaps they will take wing, and light upon our coasts. When the cranes thus begin to flutter, it is time for pygmies to keep their eyes about them. The Great Orator observes, that they will be very fit, after they have been taxed, to impose chains upon us. If they are so fit as their friend describes them, and so willing as they describe themselves, let us increase our army, and double our militia.

It has been of late a very general practice to talk of slavery among those who are setting at defiance every power that keeps the world in order. If the learned author

author of the *Reflections on Learning* has rightly observed, that no man ever could give law to language, it will be vain to prohibit the use of the word *slavery*; but I could wish it more discreetly uttered; it is driven at one time too hard into our ears by the loud hurricane of Pennsylvanian eloquence, and at another glides too cold into our hearts by the soft conveyance of a female patriot bewailing the miseries of her *friends and fellow-citizens*.

SUCH has been the progress of sedition, that those who a few years ago disputed only our right of laying taxes, now question the validity of every act of legislation. They consider themselves as emancipated from obedience, and as being no longer the subjects of the British Crown. They leave us no choice but of yielding or conquering, of resigning our dominion, or maintaining it by force.

FROM

From force many endeavours have been ufed, either to diffuade, or to deter us. Sometimes the merit of the Americans is exalted, and fometimes their fufferings are aggravated. We are told of their contributions to the laft war, a war incited by their outcries, and continued for their protection, a war by which none but themfelves were gainers. All that they can boaft is, that they did fomething for themfelves, and did not wholly ftand inactive, while the fons of Britain were fighting in their caufe.

If we cannot admire, we are called to pity them; to pity thofe that fhew no regard to their mother-country; have obeyed no law which they could violate; have imparted no good which they could withhold; have entered into affociations of fraud to rob their creditors; and into combinations to diftrefs all who depended on their commerce. We are reproached with the cruelty of fhutting one port, where

every

every port is ſhut againſt us. We are cenſured as tyrannical for hindering thoſe from fiſhing, who have condemned our merchants to bankruptcy and our manufacturers to hunger.

OTHERS perſuade us to give them more liberty, to take off reſtraints, and relax authority; and tell us what happy conſequences will ariſe from forbearance: How their affections will be conciliated, and into what diffuſions of beneficence their gratitude will luxuriate. They will love their friends. They will reverence their protectors. They will throw themſelves into our arms, and lay their property at our feet. They will buy from no other what we can ſell them; they will ſell to no other what we wiſh to buy.

THAT any obligations ſhould overpower their attention to profit, we have known them long enough not to expect. It is not to be expected from a more liberal people.

With

With what kindneſs they repay benefits, they are now ſhewing us, who, as ſoon as we have delivered them from France, are defying and proſcribing us.

BUT if we will permit them to tax themſelves, they will give us more than we require. If we proclaim them independent, they will during pleaſure pay us a ſubſidy. The conteſt is not now for money, but for power. The queſtion is not how much we ſhall collect, but by what authority the collection ſhall be made.

THOSE who find that the Americans cannot be ſhewn in any form that may raiſe love or pity, dreſs them in habiliments of terrour, and try to make us think them formidable. The Boſtonians can call into the field ninety thouſand men. While we conquer all before us, new enemies will riſe up behind, and our work will be always to begin. If we take poſſeſſion of the towns, the Coloniſts will retire into the inland regions, and the gain of victory will be only empty houſes and a wide extent of waſte and deſolation. If we ſubdue them for the preſent, they will univerſally revolt in the next war, and reſign us without pity to ſubjection and deſtruction.

To all this it may be anſwered, that between loſing America and reſigning it, there is no great difference; that it is not very reaſonable to jump into the ſea, becauſe the ſhip is leaky. All thoſe evils may befal us, but we need not haſten them.

The Dean of Glouceſter has propoſed, and ſeems to propoſe it ſeriouſly, that we ſhould at once releaſe our claims, declare them maſters of themſelves, and whiſtle them down the wind. His opinion is, that our gain from them will be the ſame, and our expence leſs. What they can have moſt cheaply from Britain, they will ſtill buy, what they can ſell to us at the higheſt price they will ſtill ſell.

It is, however, a little hard, that having ſo lately fought and conquered for their ſafety, we ſhould govern them no longer. By letting them looſe before the war, how many millions might have been ſaved. One wild propoſal is beſt anſwered by another. Let us reſtore to the French what we have taken from them. We ſhall ſee our Coloniſts at our feet, when they have an enemy ſo near them. Let us give the Indians arms, and teach them diſcipline, and encourage them now and then to plunder a Plantation. Security and leiſure are the parents of ſedition.

While theſe different opinions are agitated, it ſeems to be determined by the Legiſlature, that force ſhall be tried. Men of the pen have ſeldom any great ſkill in conquering kingdoms, but they have ſtrong inclination to give advice. I cannot forbear to wiſh, that this commotion may end without bloodſhed, and that the rebels may be ſubdued by terrour rather than by violence; and therefore recommend ſuch a force as may take away, not only the power, but the hope of reſiſtance, and by conquering without a battle, ſave many from the ſword.

If their obſtinacy continues without actual hoſtilities, it may perhaps be mollified by turning out the ſoldiers to free quarters, forbidding any perſonal cruelty or hurt. It has been propoſed, that the ſlaves ſhould be ſet free, an act which ſurely the lovers of liberty cannot but commend. If they are furniſhed with fire-arms for defence, and utenſils for huſbandry, and ſettled in ſome ſimple form of government within the country, they may be more grateful and honeſt than their maſters.

FAR be it from any Engliſhman to thirſt for the blood of his fellow-ſubjects. Thoſe who moſt deſerve our reſentment are unhappily at leſs diſtance. The Americans, when the Stamp Act was firſt propoſed, undoubtedly diſliked it, as every nation diſlikes an impoſt; but they had no thought of reſiſting it, till they were encouraged and incited by European intelligence from men whom they thought their friends, but who were friends only to themſelves.

ON the original contrivers of miſchief let an inſulted nation pour out its vengeance. With whatever deſign they have inflamed this pernicious conteſt, they are themſelves equally deteſtable. If they wiſh ſucceſs to the Colonies, they are traitors to this country, if they wiſh their defeat, they are traitors at once to America and England. To them and them only must be imputed the interruption of commerce, and the miseries of war, the sorrow of those that shall be ruined, and the blood of those that shall fall.

SINCE the Americans have made it necessary to subdue them, may they be subdued with the least injury possible to their persons and their possessions. When they are reduced to obedience, may that obedience be secured by stricter laws and stronger obligations.

NOTHING can be more noxious to society, than that erroneous clemency, which, when a rebellion is suppressed, exacts no forfeiture and establishes no securities, but leaves the rebels in their former state. Who would not try the experiment which promises advantage without expence? If rebels once obtain a victory, their wishes are accomplished; if they are defeated, they suffer little, perhaps less than their conquerors; however often they play the game,

game, the chance is always in their favour. In the mean time, they are growing rich by victualing the troops that we have sent against them, and perhaps gain more by the residence of the army than they lose by the obstruction of their port.

THEIR charters being now, I suppose, legally forfeited, may be modelled as shall appear most commodious to the Mother-country. Thus the privileges, which are found by experience liable to misuse, will be taken away, and those who now bellow as patriots, bluster as soldiers, and domineer as legislators, will sink into sober merchants and silent planters, peaceably diligent, and securely rich.

BUT there is one writer, and perhaps many who do not write, to whom the contraction of these pernicious privileges appears very dangerous, and who startle at the thoughts of *England free and America*

in

in chains. Children fly from their own shadow, and rhetoricians are frighted by their own voices. *Chains* is undoubtedly a dreadful word; but perhaps the masters of civil wisdom may discover some gradations between chains and anarchy. Chains need not be put upon those who will be restrained without them. This contest may end in the softer phrase of English Superiority and American Obedience.

We are told, that the subjection of Americans may tend to the diminution of our own liberties: an event, which none but very perspicacious politicians are able to foresee. If slavery be thus fatally contagious, how is it that we hear the loudest yelps for liberty among the drivers of negroes?

But let us interrupt a while this dream of conquest, settlement, and supremacy. Let us remember that being to contend, according

according to one orator, with three millions of Whigs, and according to another, with ninety thousand patriots of Massachuset's Bay, we may possibly be checked in our career of reduction. We may be reduced to peace upon equal terms, or driven from the western continent, and forbidden to violate a second time the happy borders of the land of liberty. The time is now perhaps at hand, which Sir Thomas Brown predicted between jest and earnest,

When America shall no more send out her treasure,
But spend it at home in American pleasure.

If we are allowed upon our defeat to stipulate conditions, I hope the treaty of Boston will permit us to import into the confederated Cantons such products as they do not raise, and such manufactures as they do not make, and cannot buy cheaper from other nations, paying like others the appointed customs; that if an English ship salutes

ſalutes a fort with four guns, it ſhall be anſwered at leaſt with two; and that if an Engliſhman be inclined to hold a plantation, he ſhall only take an oath of allegiance to the reigning powers, and be ſuffered, while he lives inoffenſively, to retain his own opinion of Engliſh rights, unmoleſted in his conſcience by an oath of abjuration.

THE END.

www.ingramcontent.com/pod-product-compliance
Lightning Source LLC
Chambersburg PA
CBHW030354270326
41926CB00009B/1100
9783744709460